THINK. PLAY. ACHIEVE!

Achieve! is a research-based series for young learners. It was designed by Houghton Mifflin Harcourt, a global leader in education serving 60 million students worldwide.

WHY IS THIS BOOK DIFFERENT?

There are hundreds of opportunities to practice skills in 4 key disciplines: math, language arts, science, and social studies.

Activities are based on new educational standards that emphasize problem-solving. This leads to higher-order thinking. That's when kids take what they've learned to solve *real-life* problems, or create something new.

Activities are also nested in topics that matter to kids: animals, Mars, and fruit smoothies. Achieve! looks like a magazine, not school work. World-class photography makes pages FIZZ.

NOW SAY SOMETHING ABOUT ME!

Oh, yes. This is Cosmo. He's on hand (and he has five of them) to help

Cover and Front Matter *cover* lion ©Shutterstock; *inside front cover:* umbrella ©Getty Images; *inside back cover:* NASA patch ©NASA; *back cover:* antique camera ©Getty Images; 3 lion ©Shutterstock; 4 rubber duck ©Shutterstock; 6 teddy bear ©Shutterstock. **Chapter 1** 8 flamingo; dog; brown bear ©Getty Images; insect; bug ©Shutterstock; butterfly ©Cutcaster; 9 beach ©Corbis; doll; passport; kangaroo ©Getty Images; feather ©Shutterstock; tractor ©Alamy Images; 10 popcorn; toy monkey; pogo stick; mask; partiers; maracas; mower ©Getty Images; 11 carrots; king; fish; pink flower; cave ©Getty Images; fox cub ©Shutterstock; pattern ©Alamy Images; 12 luggage; scooter; roller skate; train; truck; red boat ©Getty Images; 13 vase ©Getty Images; walrus ©Cutcaster; 14 apple; cut cake; bell; can; cat; pig ©Getty Images; sun ©Shutterstock; 15 apron; tractor; rake; shakes; monkey; acorns ©Getty Images; lake ©Corbis; 16 bell; flower; pig; eggplant ©Getty Images; tarantula ©Alamy Images; elephant ©Alamy Images; 17 goose ©Getty Images; 18 snake; mitt; boy; dancer ©Getty Images; dog in snow ©Alamy Images; 19 cake with swirl; drum; dice ©Getty Images; beach ©Corbis; bicycle ©iStockphoto; 20 rope; spinning top; dog ©Getty Images; 21 blue boat; nose; blue sock; truck ©Getty Images; 22 water; sunset; emu; music notes ©Getty Images; bug ©Shutterstock; 23 hat; teacup; butterfly; volleyball; bug; duck; skunk ©Getty Images; 24 ship ©Getty Images; 25 cheese ©Getty Images; chocolates ©Getty Images; 26 green snake; yellow snake; skunk; sponge ©Getty Images; snail ©Fotolia; sloth ©Alamy Images; spider ©Corbis; 27 assorted fruit; crown; pretzel ©Getty Images; blue frog ©Superstock; 28 plane; plane; sky; flowers; sled ©Getty Images; 29 sled; crab; boy; bed ©Getty Images; bird; web ©Shutterstock; 30 sand; giraffe; owl boy; mouse; monkey; plaid ©Getty Images; snake ©Shutterstock; dog ©Alamy Images; 32 bug ©Shutterstock; plaid ©Getty Images; 33 hot dog; sunset; tent ©Getty Images; 34 cake with drizzle; snail; brain ©Getty Images; crab; gold bars ©Getty Images; bacteria; grass; rock ©Shutterstock; giraffe ©Alamy Images; 36 lime; key lime pie; road ©Getty Images; boy thinking ©Fotolia; 37 road; house ©Getty Images; suit ©Shutterstock; 38 strawberry; costume; bugs; binoculars; crying baby ©Getty Images; horse ©Alamy Images; 39 baseball players ©Getty Images; balloons ©Alamy Images; 40 bricks ©Corbis; plane; grapes ©Getty Images; glue ©Alamy Images. **Chapter 2** 42 cat; mouse ©Getty Images; 43 iguana ©Getty Images; 44 boy jumping ©Getty Images; 45 kids in snow ©Alamy Images; 48 soup ©Getty Images; 50 boy on bike; girl singing ©Shutterstock; runner; boy jumping ©Getty Images; 51 painting; dancer ©Getty Images; boy with drums ©Corbis; 52 sink; kitchen; rug ©Getty Images; 53 classroom; flag ©Getty Images; building ©Shutterstock; 54 pie; apple; milk; corn; carrots; eggs; basket; cheese; pear ©Getty Images; watermelon ©Fotolia; grass ©Shutterstock; 55 kid with trophy; scowling boy; smiley face; girl with books; kids; sick boy; dog sleeping ©Getty Images; 56 boot; lamp; fish; family; shell; octopus; flag; plum; snail; unicorn; robot ©Getty Images. **Chapter 3** 58 brownstones; bulldog; kid in stroller ©Getty Images; 59 brownstones; girl with ice cream; cat; mailbox; kite ©Getty Images; red balloon ©Corbis; 60 fish tank ©Shutterstock; birdcage ©Getty Images; 61 yellow bird ©Shutterstock; hamster ©Alamy Images; cat ©Getty Images; turtle ©Getty Images; 62 grapes; broccoli; celery; carrots; bananas; apples ©Getty Images; oranges ©Alamy Images; 63 cart ©Getty Images; 64 hot chocolate; barn; skis ©Getty Images; 65 tent; sign ©Getty Images; house ©Alamy Images; cactus ©Corbis; 66 kids on bus ©Corbis; 67 bus ©Getty Images; 68 trapeze artists ©Alamy Images; hula hoop ©Corbis; 69 hula hoop ©Corbis; 70 mouse ©Getty Images; elephant; blue sneakers ©Alamy Images; 71 lamp; fish ©Shutterstock; boy sulking; snake ©Getty Images; boy smiling ©Alamy Images; 72 cactus; apple; glue; skunk ©Getty Images; 73 coins ©Shutterstock; hot chocolate; banana peel; mirror ©Getty Images; 75 rocket ©Shutterstock; 76 owl ©Getty Images; 77 chair; blanket ©Getty Images; 78 alarm clock; girl yawning ©Getty Images; 79 backpack ©Getty Images; 80 red book ©Alamy Images; 81 cityscape ©Corbis; 82 girl thinking ©Getty Images; 83 Lincoln Memorial ©Getty Images. **Chapter 4** 86 snake ©Corbis; 87 snake ©Corbis; 88 elephant ©Alamy Images; 89 elephant ©Alamy Images; 90 ukulele ©Getty Images; 91 ukulele ©Getty Images; 92 ocean cliffs ©Corbis; 93 ocean cliffs ©Corbis; 94 dollar bill ©U.S. Bureau of Engraving and Printing; karate outfit; trophy; cookie ©Getty Images; 95 karate outfit ©Getty Images; cookie ©Getty Images; 96 gumdrops ©Shutterstock; chocolates; jellybeans; fruit slices; peppermints; pink striped candy ©Getty Images; 97 gumdrops ©Shutterstock; chocolates; jellybeans; fruit slices; peppermints; candy ©Getty Images; 98 cat and mouse; frog ©Getty Images; 99 cat and mouse ©Getty Images; 100 carrot ©Shutterstock; donkey ©Getty Images; 101 pig ©Getty Images; mole ©Shutterstock; 102 pig; donkey ©Getty Images; carrot ©Shutterstock; 103 carrot ©Shutterstock; donkey ©Getty Images; 104 worm; stack of books ©Getty Images. **Chapter 5** 108 sneakers ©Getty Images; 109 baseball; cat ©Getty Images; 110 party girl; skydiver; jockey ©Getty Images; 111 skier ©Getty Images; leopard ©Corbis; 112 family laughing ©Getty Images; 113 family laughing ©Getty Images; 114 planet ©JPL/NASA; 115 galaxy ©Shutterstock; 116 dog in snow ©Getty Images; boy blowing bubble ©Alamy Images; 118 passport; sunglasses; luggage ©Getty Images; 119 luggage ©Getty Images; plane ©Shutterstock; 120 chimpanzee ©Getty Images; hyena ©Corbis; 121 alligator ©Fotolia; bat ©Getty Images; 122 penguins ©Getty Images; fire truck ©Shutterstock; 123 train ©Fotolia; chicken ©Getty Images; 124 rainbow ©Corbis; 125 wolf ©Corbis; 128 broken pencil ©Getty Images. **Chapter 6** 130 frog ©Shutterstock; rabbit ©Getty Images; 131 shell; sand dollar; pail; starfish ©Getty Images; 132 multi-colored ball ©Corbis; toy car; robot; baseball; robot; basketball; black car; robot ©Getty Images; soccer ball ©Shutterstock; toy car ©Alamy Images; 134 crown; girl in yellow ©Getty Images; 135 stack of books; rolling pin ©Getty Images; 136 cake; birthday cake ©Getty Images; 137 pineapple; coconut; parrot ©Getty Images; scorpion ©Alamy Images; 138 gems; toy chest ©Getty Images; rubber duck ©Corbis; 140 magician ©Corbis; 141 top hat ©SuperStock; 142 goldfish ©Alamy Images; 143 piggy bank; quarter ©Getty Images; 144 fish ©Shutterstock; shark ©Alamy Images; seahorse ©Getty Images; 145 broccoli; soybeans ©Getty Images; 146 boy sleeping ©Getty Images; 147 Ferris wheel ©Corbis; 150 rabbit ©Getty Images; 152 blue balloon; yellow balloon ©Getty Images; 153 multi-colored ball ©Corbis; 154 cookies; mouse ©Getty Images; 155 marbles ©Getty Images; 157 cat; birds ©Shutterstock; 158 tassel; hat with propeller; pink hat; cowboy hat; blue hat; top hat; party hat; hard hat ©Getty Images; 159 hat; hat with horns; blue hat; hat with feather; pink hat; chef hat ©Getty Images; 160 bugs; worms; snails; hedgehog ©Getty Images. **Chapter 7** 162 maracas ©Alamy Images; guitar ©Getty Images; 163 cat; animal fur ©Alamy Images; hamster; guinea pig ©Getty Images; 164 penguin; hen; goose ©Getty Images; duck ©Alamy Images; 165 robot ©Getty Images; 167 spoon ©Getty Images; 168 police badge ©Getty Images; 170 starfish ©Alamy Images; shell ©Getty Images. **Chapter 8** 180 planet ©Getty Images; sun and earth ©Age Fotostock; stars in sky ©Shutterstock; 183 peanut; toy soldier ©Getty Images; grasshopper ©Shutterstock; 184 bird ©Shutterstock; 186 cheese ©Getty Images; 188 place setting ©Getty Images; 200 eyeball ©Corbis; 201 leaf ©Shutterstock. **Chapter 9** 202 rat; lizard ©Getty Images; 203 pencil; paper clip; wand; ladybug ©Getty Images; 204 pig; goat ©Getty Images; dog ©Alamy Images; 205 chameleon; bird ©Getty Images; goldfish ©Alamy Images; 210 boy in mirror; girl brushing teeth ©Getty Images; boy eating dinner ©Alamy Images; kid at beach ©Shutterstock. **Chapter 10** 217 robot ©Getty Images; 218 alphabet blocks; cans; boy with beach ball ©Getty Images; 219 cheese ©Getty Images; party hat ©Shutterstock; milk ©Alamy Images; 226 apple; ice cream; slice; wafer; hot dog ©Getty Images; 227 dog ©Getty Images; wood ©Shutterstock; 228 pizza slice ©Alamy Images; 236 cookies ©Getty Images. **Chapter 11** 232 girl on phone; boy reading; cat; fork ©Getty Images; girl holding nose ©Alamy Images; 233 baby ©Getty Images; 234 fish bowl; bug; thermometer; pizza slice; guinea pig ©Getty Images; 235 beakers ©Alamy Images; screwdriver; scissors; measuring spoons; tape measure; wooden spoon; shovel; hand mixer; rolling pin; hammer; binoculars; nose ©Getty Images; hands ©Shutterstock. **Chapter 12** 238 frog; goldfish ©Alamy Images; feathers ©Corbis; parrot; porcupine; brass; snakeskin ©Getty Images; insect ©Shutterstock; 240 spider ©Corbis; skunk; prairie dog; beavers ©Getty Images; fish ©Alamy Images; 241 flowers; plant; rocks ©Getty Images; rabbit; baby birds ©Alamy Images; 242 sign ©Cutcaster; tiger ©Getty Images. **Chapter 13** 253 mailbox ©Getty Images; 254 planet ©Shutterstock; 255 water fountain; window shutter; lemons ©Getty Images; egg ©Corbis; swimmer ©Shutterstock; plant ©Alamy Images; 256 sunrays ©Shutterstock; shark; sun through water; fish ©Alamy Images; 258 tub; hose ©Getty Images; creek ©Shutterstock; toothbrush ©Alamy Images; 259 people rowing ©Alamy Images; 260 car on road; oil slick ©Getty Images; bird; fish ©Shutterstock; 261 toothbrush ©Alamy Images; 262 soil ©Shutterstock; corn ©Corbis; 263 boat ©Getty Images; boy on bike ©Shutterstock; 265 trees ©Alamy Images; sun and clouds ©Getty Images; clouds ©Shutterstock. **Chapter 14** 269 bubble mix; orange juice; purple balloon ©Getty Images; 270 doorbell; boy on scooter; shopping cart ©Getty Images; kids playing ©Alamy Images; lifeguard ©Corbis; 271 ambulance; piano; fire detector; door ©Getty Images; bicycle ©Shutterstock. **Chapter 15** 286 Christmas ornaments ©Corbis; 289 street sign ©Getty Images; 298 shoes ©Getty Images; 302 peanut butter; peanut butter and jelly ©Getty Images. **Chapter 16** 304 girl at dentist; barber; mechanic ©Getty Images; dog walker ©Alamy Images; 305 cereal; cereal box ©Getty Images; 306 dog bone ©Getty Images; wood ©Shutterstock; 307 muffin ©Getty Images; 308 purple balloon; purse; flowerpot; champagne ©Getty Images; 309 wrench ©Getty Images; lemonade; sunflowers ©Alamy Images. **Stickers** red flower ©Getty Images, oranges ©Getty Images, starfish ©Getty Images, bird ©Shutterstock, turtle ©Alamy Images, sneakers ©Getty Images, butterfly ©Alamy Images, blue frog ©SuperStock, grapes ©Getty Images, purple flower ©Getty Images.

Send all inquiries to: Permissions, The Learning Company, 222 Berkeley Street, Boston, Massachusetts, 02116-3748

ISBN: 9780544372610

www.hmhco.com

Manufactured in the United States of America

DOM 10 9 8 7 6 5 4 3 2 1

4500478014

ACHIEVE!

Edited by Sharon Emerson and Meredith Phillips

Houghton Mifflin Harcourt

Boston   New York

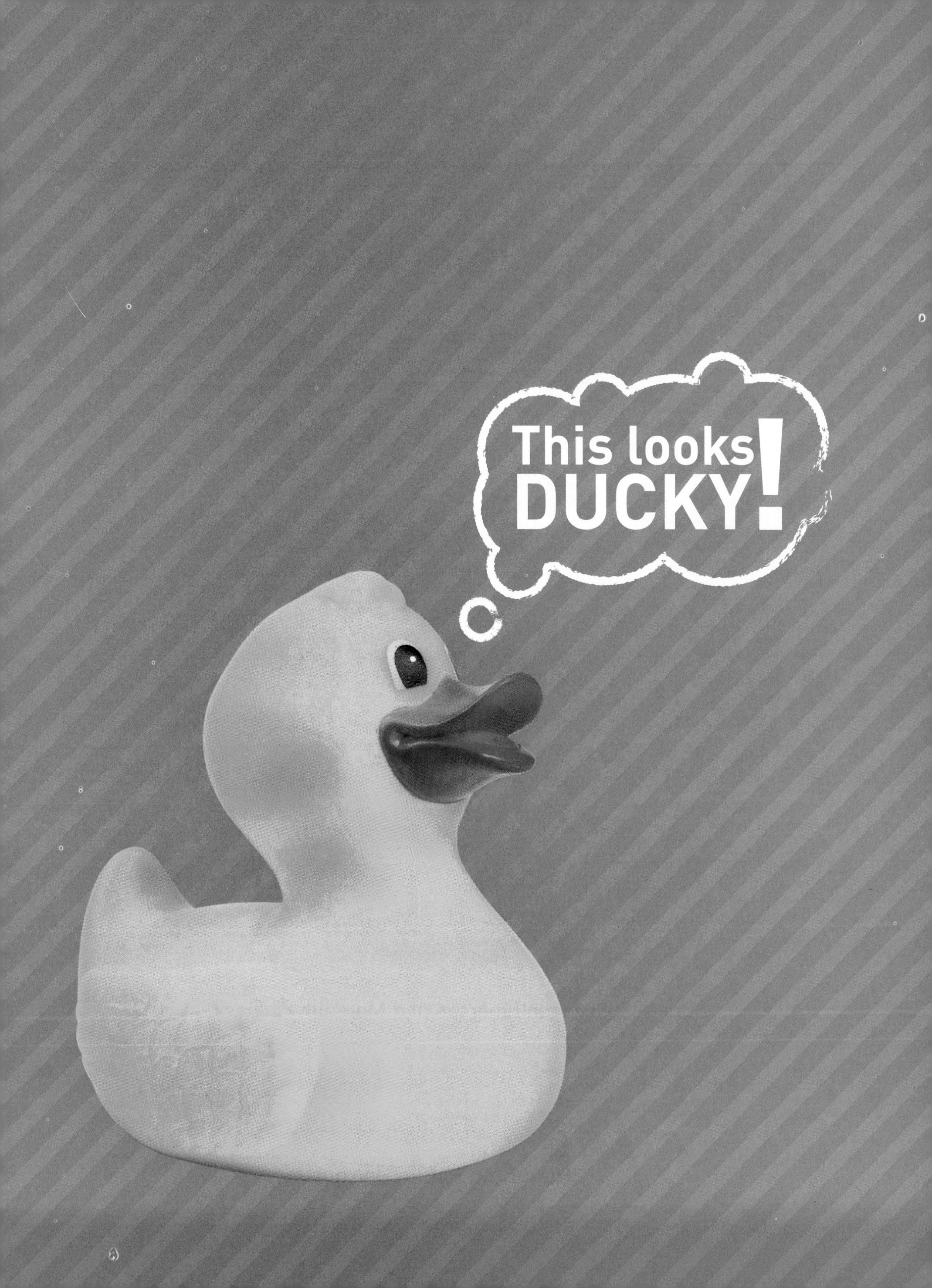
This looks
DUCKY!

Contents

Phonics 7

Spelling and Vocabulary 41

Grammar and Mechanics 57

Reading 85

Writing 105

Addition and Subtraction 129

Math Facts 161

Number and Operations. 171

Measurement and Data 201

Geometry 215

Nature of Science 231

Life Science 237

Earth Science 251

Physical Science 267

Community 273

Marketplace 303

Answer Key 311

Phonics

Big Dark Forest

The forest is full of creatures that start with b, d, or f sounds. Say the name of each animal. What sound does it begin with? Write the letter.

Hop, Jump, Kick!

Help Kanga Kit <u>h</u>op, <u>j</u>ump, and <u>k</u>ick her way to Baby Roo! Draw a line through pictures that start with **h**, **j**, or **k**.

You're Invited!

Welcome to a _mighty _loud _party! Everyone brings something that starts with m, l, or p. Say the name of each item. What sound does it start with? Write the letter.

What **m**, **l**, or **p** thing will you bring to the party?

The fox needs to get back to his den. *Quickly!* Draw a line through pictures that start with **q** to get him there.

Quick
Like a Fox!

Q and U stick like glue! Most **q** words are followed by a **u**. Can you think of any? *Don't worry!* This isn't a quiz.

Rail, Stream, Trail

Take a trip to a faraway place! But how will you get there? Each option starts with **r**, **s**, or **t**. Say the word out loud. What sound does it start with? **Write the letter.**

Wacky Birthday to You!

Say the name of each gift. Then match the sound it starts with to a letter.

v   w   x   y   z

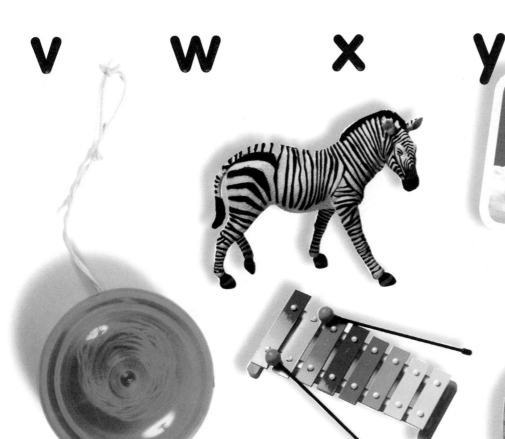

What? You already have a _walrus? Choose a different word that starts with a **w** sound.

_____

I want a **w** _____.

Anteater Antics

Alice Anteater collects things that begin with a **short a**, like ant.

Say the words below. Circle the words with a **short a**.

Aping Around

April the <u>A</u>pe loves the **a** sound, too. But she collects words with a **long a**, like <u>a</u>pe.

Say the words below. Circle the words with a **long a**.

Essie **Is Excellent!**

Essie is an excellent elephant! She smells a snack! Lead her to the berries. Draw a line through pictures that make **short e** sounds.

An elephant can use its trunk to pick up tiny things. Like berries!

Gene loves to take pictures of animals. The more elusive, the better! He is trying to find an Egyptian egret. The bird is across the river. Color in stones with **long e** sounds to make a path for Gene.

The
Egret
of
Egypt

bee

nest

egg

bird

tree

boat

boot

deer

sock

Dizzy Izzy

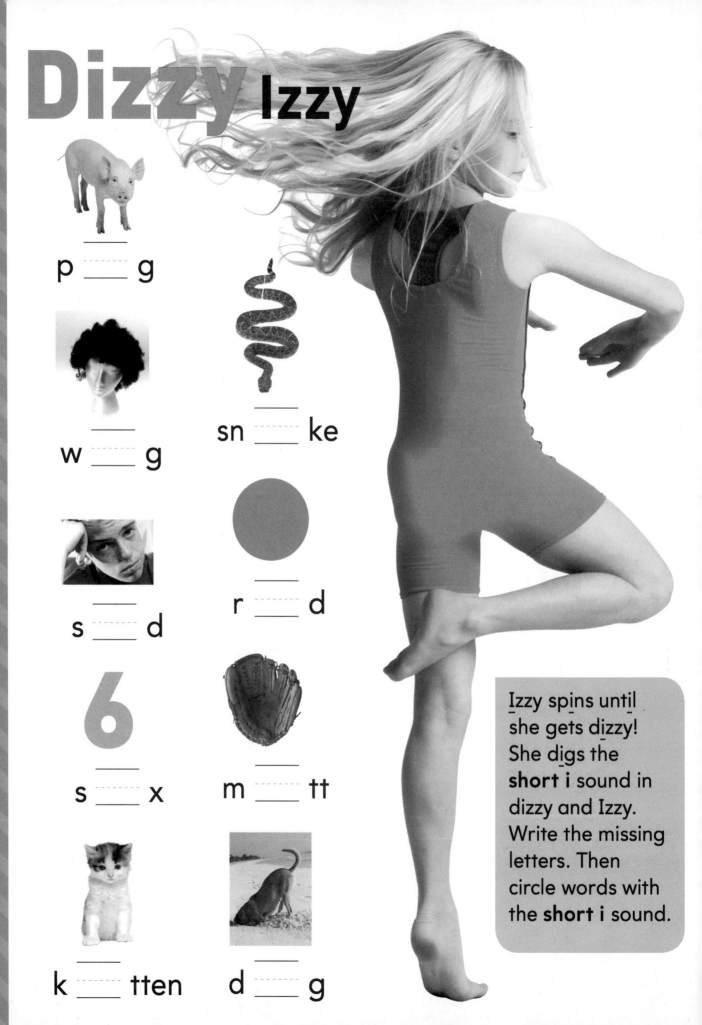

p _ g

w _ g

sn _ ke

s _ d

r _ d

6

s _ x

m _ tt

k _ tten

d _ g

Izzy spins until she gets dizzy! She digs the **short i** sound in dizzy and Izzy. Write the missing letters. Then circle words with the **short i** sound.

Ice, Ice, Ivy!

Ivy slides on the ice. She thinks it sounds nice!
Write the missing letters. Then circle words
with the **long i** sound.

 k ___ te

 l ___ ps

 ___ ce

 dr ___ m

 d ___ ce

 b ___ ke

 m ___ g

 m ___ ce

c ___ ke

Ollie Ox and

Ollie Ox and Owen Okapi are having a rhyming contest. Help them complete their rhymes! Match the **short o** words that rhyme.

flop, pop, _____

dot, cot, _____

rock, sock, _____

hog, frog, _____

Start a rhyming bee at dinner! Is that *fish* in your *dish*? Is that a *roll* in your *bowl*? Is that a *cucumber* in your *tumbler*?

Owen Okapi

Match the **long o** words that rhyme.

flow, row, _____

oh, no, _____

oat, goat, _____

rose, toes, _____

Lucy the Whale

Lucy the Whale sings *Blue! Blue! Blue!* because she loves the **long u**!

Say the words below. Write the missing letters. Then circle words with the **long u** sound.

j __ __ ice

r __ __ ler

c __ __ p

m __ __ sic

s __ __ n

b __ __ g

em __ __

c __ __ be

Thunderstorm!

It's raining words! Circle words with short u sounds. Then write them under the umbrella to keep them dry!

ball bug butterfly duck hat pig skunk teacup truck

Chomp. Thump.

____ erry

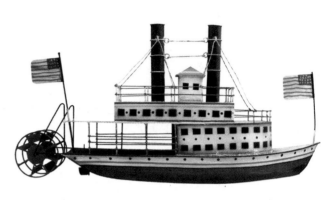

____ ip

____ rone

____ ree

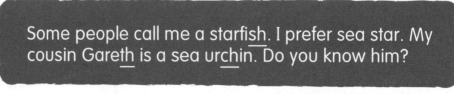

Some people call me a starfish. I prefer sea star. My cousin Gareth is a sea urchin. Do you know him?

Shhh!

Say the word for each picture. Do you hear a **ch**, **th**, or **sh** sound? Write the missing letters.

____ eese

____ ade

____ ocolate

____ apes

When I'm hungry, I push my stomach outside of my mouth. I told Gareth. He thinks I'm lying. But it's the truth!

S Pals

One is <u>s</u>low. Another is <u>s</u>limy. *Pee-ew!* That one is <u>s</u>melly!

Say the name of each creature. Circle the letters that make the beginning sound. Then write one of the words to describe it.

scaly   scary   slimy   slow   smelly   springy

sn   sp   st   sn   sn   sk

_____   _____   _____

st   sp   sl   sp   sk   sp

_____   _____   _____

Some letters work together to make a new sound. S teams up with **c, k, l, m, n, p, t,** and **w**. My favorite team is **st** as in <u>st</u>ar. Sea <u>st</u>ar!

26

Friendly R

R has letter buddies, too! Say the word for each picture. **Circle the letters that make the beginning sound.**

fr   cr

tr   gr

dr   tr

pr   cr

cr   fr

fr   dr

I know who drives that truck! It's Patrice. She travels with a frog named Prince. They deliver fruit and pretzels to grocery stores!

The Play Must Go On!

Clara and Placido wrote a play. They call it *The Pleasant Playground*. The class made props. Circle the letters that make the beginning sound of each prop.

cl pl

pl sl

sl cl

pl sl

sl fl

Please clap if you liked the play!

Bed Head Bob!

Bed Head Bob mixed up his **b**'s and **d**'s. Help him sort them out! Say the word. Does it end in a **b** or **d** sound? Write the letter.

ki ___

ri ___

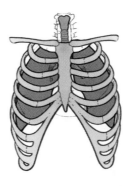

cra ___

sle ___

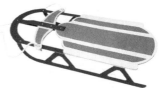

wee ___

we ___

cri ___

bir ___

WHO at the ZOO Starts With M?

Two of these animals start with the same sound. Draw a line to connect them.

Fun in the Sun!

Liam is writing words in the sand. Help him write the last letter of each word. Say the word. Does it end with an m or an n sound?

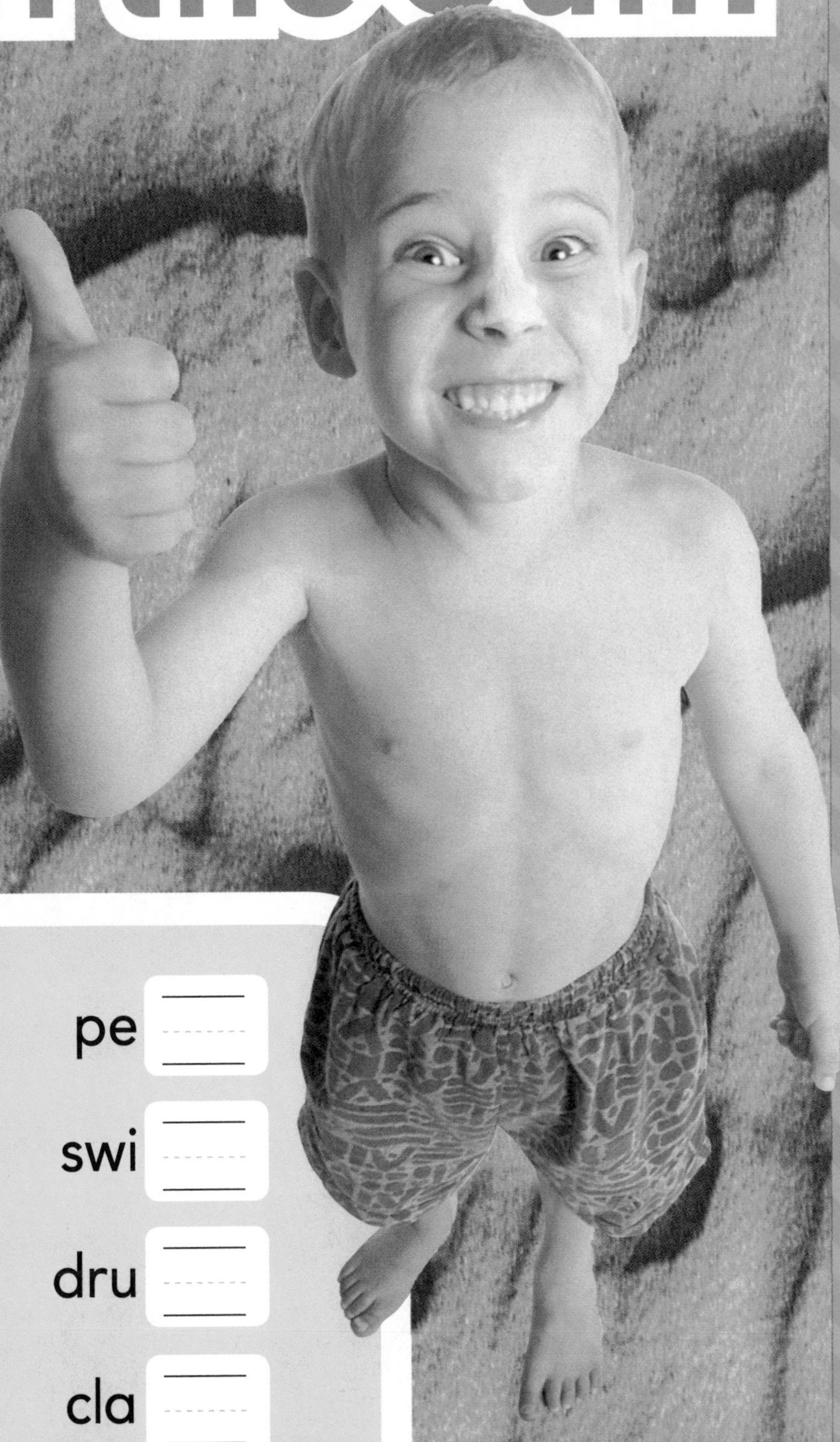

mo ____

ta ____

fa ____

ca ____

pi ____

pe ____

swi ____

dru ____

cla ____

ma ____

Camp Big Bad Wolf

The Big Bad Wolf loves to camp on the weekends!
This is his campsite. The short vowels are missing.
Write the missing vowels.

m __ p

b __ g

st __ ck

l __ g

t __ nt

s __ n

h __ t d __ g

A sea star has one long vowel sound and one short vowel.

The Yuckiest Page in This Book!
(Don't You Agree?)

Look at the yucky pictures! Write the missing words under each.

brain   cake

nail   lake

snail   plate

_____ on a _____

_____ on a _____

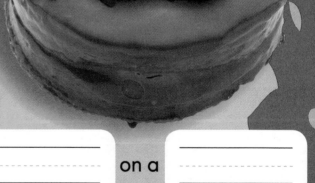

_____ on a _____

Sometimes the **long a** sound is spelled **ai** as in br**ai**n. But sometimes the **long a** sound is spelled **a_e**, as in c**a**k**e**!

City Giraffe and Country Goat

C and G make two sounds, hard and soft.

City has a **soft c**, but country has a **hard c**.
Giraffe has a **soft g**, but goat has a **hard g**.

Say each word below. **If the sound is soft, write it on a pillow. If the sound is hard, write it on a rock.**

 circle   grass   germ   city   giant   car   gold crab

soft c

hard c

soft g

hard g

Read the story below. Write in the missing words.

Once Upon a PIE

dime   fly   lime   mind   pie   sign

Manuel found a _____. He saw a

bakery _____. *I'd like a*

slice of _____! *The one made*

with _____! A _____

flew in the door. It landed on the pie! So Manuel

changed his _____.

Sometimes the **long i** sound is spelled **ie**, as in l**ie**. Sometimes it is spelled **i_e**, as in t**i**m**e**. And sometimes it is spelled with **y**, as in wh**y**.

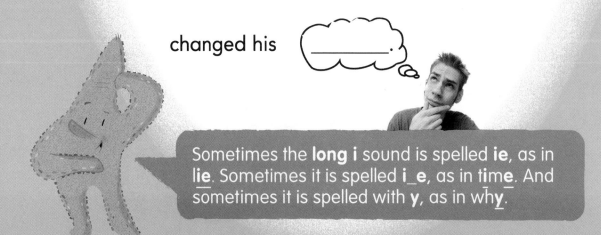

A Home for Toad

Read the story below. **Write in the missing words.**

| coat | home | nose | road | Rose | toad | toes |

The _____ lived alone. It saw a

girl across the  _____. Her name

was  _____. *Hop, hop, hop!* It stopped at

her _____. Rose picked it up and kissed

its _____. Into her _____

pocket it goes! Let's go  _____!

Sometimes the **long o** sound is spelled **o_e**, as in n**o**se. Sometimes it is spelled **oa**, as in b**oa**t.

Cry Baby!

Y likes to change sounds.

Sometimes **y** sounds like a **long i**. As in cr<u>y</u>!
Sometimes **y** sounds like a **long e**. As in bab<u>y</u>.

Say the words below. Which sound does the **y** make?
Write each word in the correct list.

berry

fly

fairy

pony

sky

spy

long i	long e
cry	baby

Balloon Dudes

cute

moon

spoon

tooth

tune

boots

blue

ue

oo

These dudes lost their balloons. **Draw a string from each balloon to the correct dude.**

Sometimes the long **u** sound is spelled with **u_e**, as in d**u**d**e**. That sound can also be spelled **oo**, as in ball**oo**n.

LETTER BLENDER

Stella and Frank are blending letters in the smoothie machine! **Add the blended letters to complete the words below.**

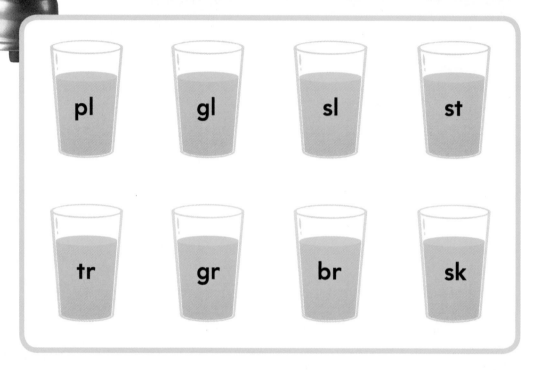

pl	gl	sl	st
tr	gr	br	sk

_____ ane

_____ ick

_____ ide

_____ ates

_____ ain

_____ ue

_____ apes

_____ ar

Spelling
and
Vocabulary

Three Nice Mice

Use these words to complete the story.

are   is   like   see   us   We

Sam _____ the cat.

We _____ mice.

We _____ Sam.

_____ play with Sam.

Sam does not eat _____!

We _____ Sam.

I ♥ My Lizard!

Use these words to complete the story.

all   does   I   He   him   me   my

- Leo is _____ lizard.

  Leo likes to play with _____

  _____ take care of _____ .

- Leo _____ a funny trick.

  Leo eats _____ the food.

  _____ is a good pet.

- What might Leo eat? Draw it.

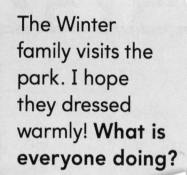

The Winter family visits the park. I hope they dressed warmly! **What is everyone doing?**

Winter Wonderland

He   her   his   it   She   Their   They

What is Mr. Winter doing?

_____ is snowboarding.

Where are _____ boys?

_____ are sledding with a friend.

The Winter girl took off _____ coat.

_____ and a friend are making a

snowman.

_____ snowman is done!

The girls name _____ . . .   _____ !

Word Soup

Danielle's alphabet soup is cold! She wants to spell words, not eat them! **How many words can you make?**

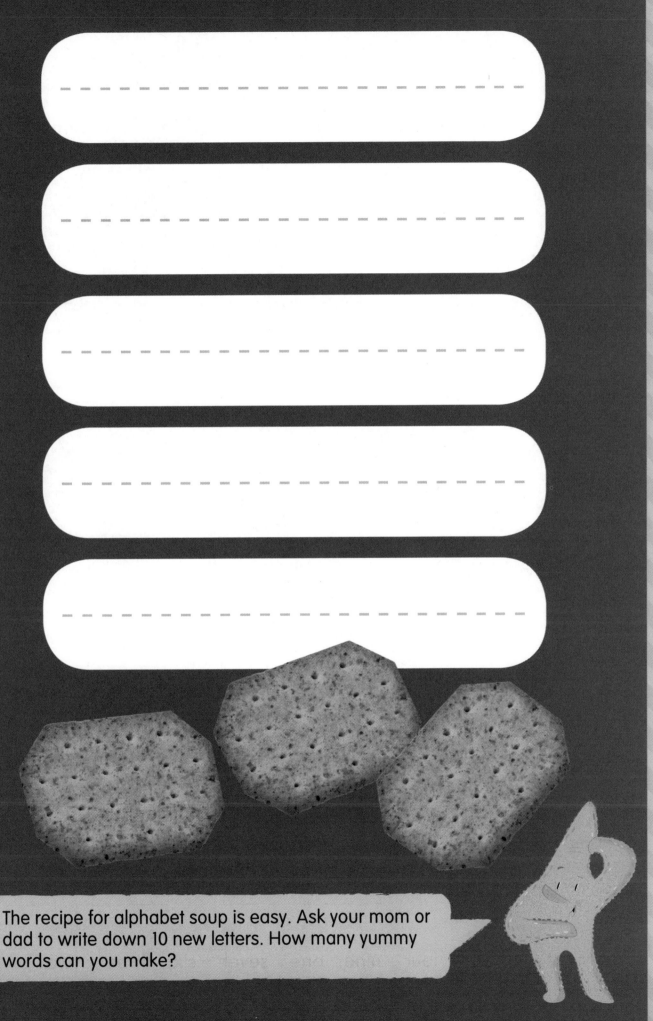

The recipe for alphabet soup is easy. Ask your mom or dad to write down 10 new letters. How many yummy words can you make?

Lucky Number

Each jersey has a number. **Write the word for each number.**

eight   five   four   nine   one   seven   six   three   two

Rainbow Words

Read the word for each color.
Then color it in to match the word!

Red Blue

Orange Purple

Yellow White

Green Black

Pink Brown

A lot of sea creatures are named after colors…the white anemone, purple-striped jellyfish, and blue whale. Can you guess the colors of a parrot fish?

The ★ Super Sullivans

The Sullivan family is very talented. Write the talent of each family member below.

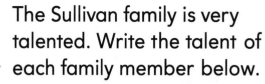

 drum  dance  sing  kick

- - - - - - - - - -

The Sullivan family wants you to star in their talent show. Write your talent in the star!

- - - - - - - - - -

- - - - - - - - - -

ride

run

paint

Home
Sweet Home

Use the photos to solve the word puzzle.

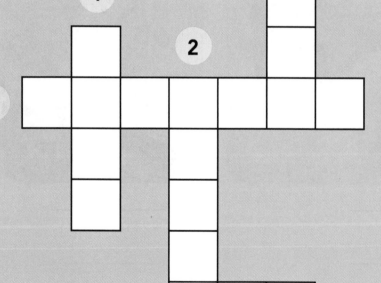

DOWN

1.

2.

3.

ACROSS

4.

5.

6.

chair   kitchen   lamp   rug   sink   table

School Search!

Can you find these school words in the picture? Draw a line from the word to the picture.

flag

teacher

student

book

backpack

pencil

The Tree

Ff

Picnic!

Find the foods shown below!

```
n q a t u i c g h r
a o c h e e s e e e
t l l m a c k k i g
o s c e o p c l p g
f t j g m a p l i s
r o f m r r y l w m
o r t c i h e c e y
d r a e p u o t j q
k a i c r r y a a i
d c b i n v s i r w
```

apple   carrots   cheese   corn   cracker
eggs   milk   pear   pie   watermelon

I Feel Fine!

Everyone is in a different mood! **Write the mood word to complete each sentence.**

Lois feels _____.

Olivia feels _____.

Theo feels _____.

Mia feels _____.

Gabe feels _____.

Milo feels _____.

Noah feels _____.

happy

sad

mad

scared

silly

sleepy

sick

How do you feel today? I am _____.

HOORAY! Today is my birthday. Guess how I feel! *Wait.*
You *forgot* it was my birthday? *Now* guess how I feel.

Don't panic! Letters are disappearing from important words! *I hpe it's nt too lte!*

Say each word. What sound is missing? **Write the missing letter.**

Case of the Missing Letter

snai ___

s ___ ell

k ___ te

___ nicorn

l ___ mp

ru ___

fi ___

___ obot

pl ___ m

fla ___

boo ___

l ___ on

___ ctopus

famil ___

What do you call a starfish with no eyes?
Starfish!

Grammar
and
Mechanics

GOING TO NOUN TOWN?

The Peabody family visits Noun Town. Noun Town is a place filled with fun people and things. **Write the names of** people **and** things **the Peabody family sees.**

balloon	boy	cat	dad
dog	girl	ice cream	kite
	mailbox		

Noun Town is nice. But I hear Thingville has better custard.

Pet Sitter!

Irma is pet sitting. Where are the pets? They are not in the usual places. **Write the words for each place.**

| aquarium | bird cage | wheel | windowsill |

Here are the pets! **Write the name of each animal.**

| canary | cat | hamster | turtle |

A SUPER

A truck delivers fruits and vegetables to the market. **Write the name of each fruit and vegetable.**

MARKET Job!

Draw a line from each food to the right cart.

apples

bananas

grapes

celery

pears

oranges

broccoli

carrots

SUMMER Vacation

Isa wants to go on vacation with her cousins.
Where are they going? **Write it in.**

| farm | desert | beach | mountains | home |

Where did Ben go?

Ben went to the _____ to ski.

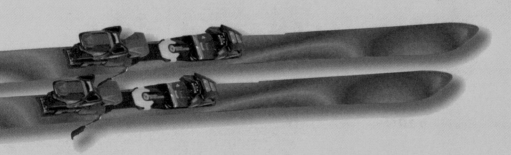

Where did Max go?

Max went to a

_____ to milk cows.

Where did Kari go?

Kari went to the _____ to surf.

Where did Mia and Marco go?

Mia and Marco went to the

_____ to hike.

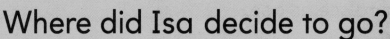

Where did Isa decide to go?

She spent summer vacation at her favorite place.

Isa stayed _____!

Field Trip!

Kim is going on a field trip to Carson Zoo. Read the story. **Circle the** proper nouns in each sentence.

"Hurry up, Kim!" Mom shouts. "You will miss the bus!"

Kim runs five blocks to Green Day School.

The bus driver, Joan, is waiting.

Kim sits next to her friend Laura.

They drive to Carson Zoo.

Kim and Laura see an ape.

Stan Bock sees it, too.

They visit the Bird House.

They see the Talking Birds show.

"I am Kim," says Kim.

"I am Kim," says the bird.

A **proper noun** starts with a capital letter. It names a person or place. I am *Cosmo*! I live off the coast of *North Carolina*.

Circle the **proper noun** in each pair below.

kid	Carly
state	North Dakota
soldier	Lieutenant Davis
Amazon	river
mountain	Mount Kilimanjaro
Statue of Liberty	statue

My favorite proper noun is _____.

Draw it!

BIG Banana

Idi visits the circus with his family.
Circle the verb **in each sentence.**
Hint: look for the action word!

The clown juggles.

The acrobat flies through the air.

The strong man lifts weights.

The lady walks on a tightrope.

The dog jumps through a hoop.

Idi cheers!

If you want to know what someone is doing,
look for the **verb**! I *sing*! I *splash*! I *swim*!
Without verbs, life would be dull.

Circus

Idi wants to join the circus. **Add verbs to tell what Idi can do!**

drive   jump   ride

Join the Big Banana Circus!

Name: _Idi C._

Age: _9_

Idi can _____ on a trampoline.

Idi can _____ a clown car.

Idi can _____ a unicycle.

Opposite Day

An **adjective** describes a noun. It's the difference between a spider and a **hairy** spider! **Write an** adjective **to describe each picture.**

> clean   dark   dry
> happy   small

big

_____
....
_____

_____
....
_____

dirty

bright _____

sad

_____

wet

_____

Do you have a boring noun? Then dress it up with an **adjective**! That is a stunning, sharp, yellow pencil! Can I borrow it?

STINKY Apple!

These adjectives describe the wrong pictures!
Write each adjective **under the right picture.**

stinky

_____

red

_____

fast

_____

prickly

_____

slippery

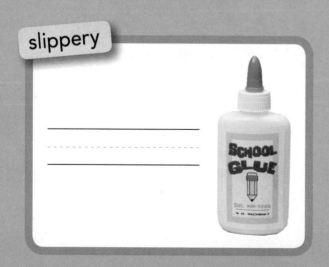

_____

SCHOOL GLUE

broken

_____
- - - - - - - - - -
_____

hot

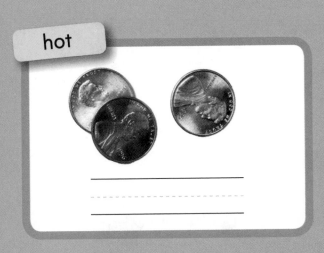

_____
- - - - - - - - - -
_____

sticky

_____
- - - - - - - - - -
_____

three

_____
- - - - - - - - - -
_____

green

_____
- - - - - - - - - -
_____

The Elephant SINGS!

Read the sentence. Circle the noun. Underline the verb.

The elephant sings.

Now rewrite the sentence.

_____

. . . .

_____

Rewrite each sentence. Capitalize the first word of each sentence. Add a period at the end of each sentence.

Then, circle the nouns. Underline the verbs.

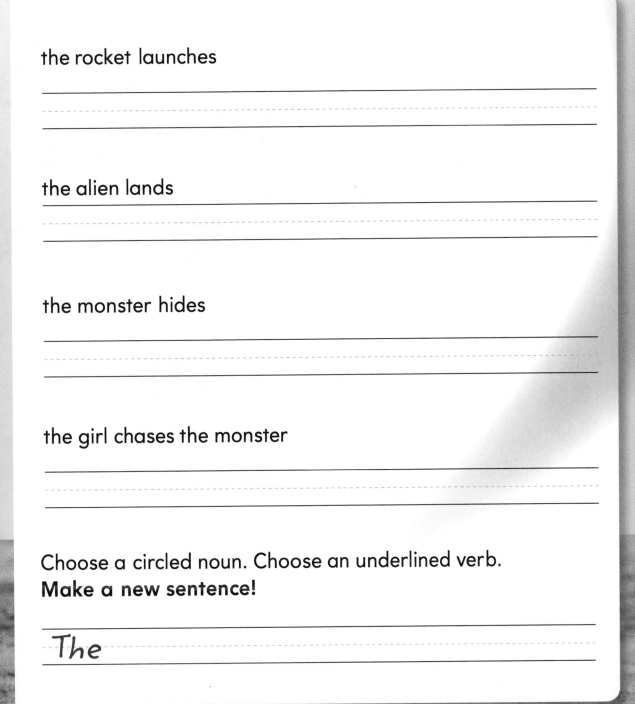

the rocket launches

the alien lands

the monster hides

the girl chases the monster

Choose a circled noun. Choose an underlined verb.
Make a new sentence!

The

Say What, Mr. Who?

Mr. Who asks a lot of questions! Read each sentence. What do you think Mr. Who asked?

Write the correct question word.

Who	What	When	Where	Why	How

This is a fort.

_____ is this?

Josh built a fort.

_____ built a fort?

He built it in his room.

_____ did he build it?

He went into the fort this afternoon.

_____ did he go into the fort?

Josh built the fort with blankets and chairs.

_____ did Josh build it?

Josh built it to hide from his sister.

_____ did Josh build it?

A question asks who, what, when, where, why, or how. 'What's for lunch?' is my favorite question. *What*? Clams again?

LIVE IN THE NOW!

Neve lives in the now! Read all the things Neve does right now. **Add s to the verb in each sentence.**

Neve wake___ up early!

Neve eat___ cereal. She clean___ her bowl!

Neve pet___ the cat.

Neve run___ out the door to get to school.

Neve laugh___ at every joke she hear___ !

Why does the zombie stay home from school?

He feel___ rotten.

BACK TO THE FUTURE!

Bing left his homework at home! He needs to go back in time to get it! **Add** ed **to each verb to make it past tense.**

Bing stepp_____ into the time machine. He travel_____ back home. He look_____ for his homework.

He found it! He grabb_____ it off the kitchen table. He stuff_____ it into his backpack. He return_____ to class. He open_____ his backpack. He hand_____ his homework to the teacher.

Seeing Double!

Mindy and Cindy are twins. They need at least two of everything! **Add s** to the words below to make them plural. Then write the word.

shoe   *shoes*

mirror   _____

backpack   _____

sweater   _____

book   _____

computer   _____

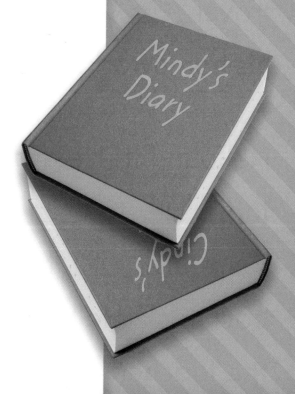

THE Spirit of St. Louis

Ishan and his family visited St. Louis. Read about the trip! **Replace nouns with** proper nouns.

Lewis and Clark

United States

St. Louis

the Gateway Arch

June

Cardinals

Ishan and his family drove to ~~the city~~ _____.

They went in ~~the summer~~ _____. They saw

~~a monument~~ _____. It is the tallest monument

in the ~~country~~ _____. It is a symbol of the

journey of ~~two explorers~~ _____. Later, Ishan's

family went to the stadium to see the ~~baseball team~~

_____. *Go team!*

Get it? Got it. GOOD!

The punctuation fell off of these sentences! How will they end? **Punctuate each sentence to end it.**

Can I have a cookie___

Look out, Jack___

I left my hat in my room___

Hooray, it's snowing___

What's for dinner___

I have a dog named Pete___

Read each sentence out loud. **Circle the one that sounds more exciting!**

I had pizza for dinner.

I had pizza for dinner!

An exclamation mark is loud. Really loud! Really, really, really loud!!!

82

Capitals at the Capital!

Barry and his sister visited the capital. He wrote a letter home. He forgot to capitalize the first letter of some sentences. **Circle them.**

Hi, Mom!

we are in Washington, D.C.

aunt Judy picked us up at the train station.

She took us to the National Mall. It sounds like a store. but it's a park.

we walked to the Lincoln Memorial. Ellen tried to sit on Lincoln's lap!

tomorrow we'll have a picnic on Capitol Hill.

i wish we could stay longer!

Love,
Barry

See Cupcakes! Eat Cupcakes!

Read the word on each cupcake.

Is it a **verb**? Draw sprinkles on it.

Is it a **noun**? Draw a cherry on top.

Is it an **adjective**? Draw extra frosting on it.

pink

fast

run

book

dog

look

sweet

ice

Reading

Sammy

Snakes are very different from people.

Sammy is a snake.

Sammy is green.

Sammy has scales. If you touch a snake, it feels smooth and strong.

Sammy does not have any legs. He can't run for the bus!

Sammy does not have hands. He can't scratch his back!

Sammy has a tongue. Snakes use their tongues to smell!

Snakes are very interesting.

Snake

Read about Sammy.

Fill in the blanks.

Sammy is a _____.

Sammy has _____.

Sammy doesn't have _____

or _____.

Sammy uses his _____ to smell.

I have five arms. But it's still hard to scratch
my own back. Can you do it? *Ahhh*.

Everett the

Everett is an elephant.

He is gray.

Everett has huge ears.

He has wrinkly skin.

He has a long trunk.

Everett's trunk can pick up leaves.

His trunk can spray water.

Everett's trunk is an important tool.

Elephant

Read about Everett. **Answer the questions.**

What is Everett?

Everett is an _____.

Circle words in the story that tell how Everett looks.

How might Everett's skin feel if you touched it?

Everett's skin might feel _____.

How is Everett's trunk a tool?

Everett's trunk can _____.

His trunk can also _____.

Una Ukulele

Una loves music.

Her parents got her a ukulele.

A ukulele looks like a small guitar.

But it only has four strings — not six.

Una plucks the ukulele with her thumb.

She plays a song. Her brother sings along.

Oh my darling, Oh my darling

Oh my darling Clementine...

Una stops playing. She's laughing too hard.

Read about Una's ukulele.
Answer the questions.

Why did Una's parents get her a ukulele?

Una _____ music.

How is a ukulele different than a guitar?

It is _____ than a guitar.

It has _____ strings.

A guitar has _____ strings.

How does Una play the ukulele?

She uses her _____.

Does Una like when her brother sings along?

Yes   No

Bronte Goes Home

I was born in Haiti.

Haiti is an island. The air is warm.

The buildings are small.

We all slept in one room.

I moved to New York when I was five.

New York is cold. We live in a tall building.

We go back to visit Haiti. We visit my cousins.

I love to see them.

Coming home to New York makes me happy and sad.

Who is telling the story?

_____ is telling the story.

Circle (words) that tell about Haiti.

Underline things that tell about New York.

Do you think Bronte likes New York?

Yes   No

Draw a picture of Bronte in New York.

The best stories make me feel happy
and sad at the same time.

How Do You

Read each sentence.
Write how each person feels.

Jens won a trophy!

excited sad

Jens is ___excited___.

Celia visited her cousins.

tired happy

Celia is _____.

Wyeth found a dollar.

surprised angry

Wyeth is _____.

Feel?

Emmett heard a loud noise.

glad frightened

Emmett feels _____.

Amelia's brother earned his yellow belt.

proud scared

Amelia feels _____.

Henry's brother took his cookie.

loved mad

Henry feels _____.

Jon took his brother's cookie.

guilty sleepy

Jon feels _____.

A Kid in a
Candy Shop

Palmer went to a candy shop.

He was amazed.

He saw jellybeans in jars.

He saw bubble gum in barrels.

He saw popcorn in paper bags.

He saw twisted taffy in a tower.

Palmer likes candy. But his favorite treat is ice cream.

Palmer went to the ice cream shop.

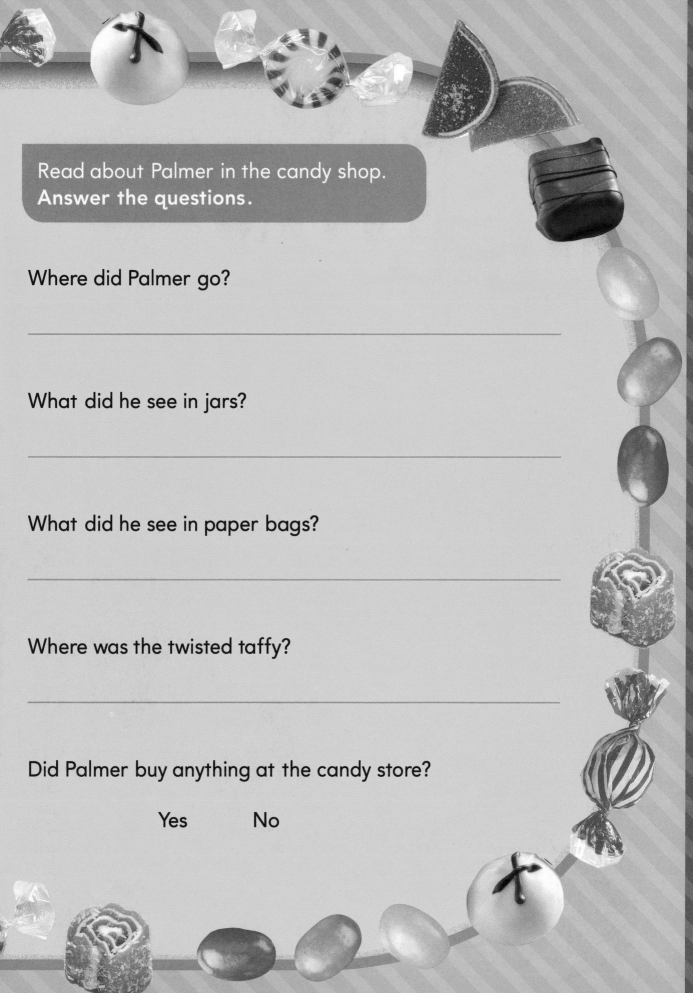

Read about Palmer in the candy shop.
Answer the questions.

Where did Palmer go?

_____

What did he see in jars?

_____

What did he see in paper bags?

_____

Where was the twisted taffy?

_____

Did Palmer buy anything at the candy store?

Yes   No

Leapin' Lenny

Lenny is a frog.

Just watch him leap!

He can jump up seven feet!

Oh! There's a cat.

Can Lenny clear it?

Of course he can.

He just won't go near it!

How high can Lenny jump?

_____

Why doesn't Lenny want to jump over the cat?

_____

_____

Draw a picture of Lenny jumping over the cat.

Many frogs can jump as high as 10 feet!
That's high for a little guy!

Mighty Mole

Mule was walking home.

He saw something in the ground.

It was green and leafy. It looked like the top of a juicy carrot!

"This is a good snack!" said Mule.

Mule grabbed it and tugged. But the food was stuck tight.

"I cannot pick it up by myself," said Mule.

So Pig came up to help him.

"Let's tie a rope around it," said Pig.

They pulled the rope together.

The food did not budge! *Not an inch!*

Mole lived underground. He heard them talking.

They tied a rope around the carrot!

"Can I help?" Mole asked.

"Don't be silly," grunted Mule.

"You are too little," gasped Pig.

But Mole had to try. He grabbed the rope.

He tugged with all his might. And…

Pop!

Little Mole had done it!

"You are a mighty fellow!" cried Pig.

"A Mighty Mole!" cheered Mule.

Who are the characters in this story?

☐ Mule, Pig, and Mole

☐ a carrot and a piece of rope

Where does this story take place?

☐ in Mole's house   ☐ outside

Retell what happened in the story. Use your own words.

Betty Bookworm

Betty loves books!

She loves to *EAT* books!

She eats every book she sees...

...big books, little books, storybooks, and textbooks.

Have you seen a book? It's lunchtime. And she's hungry!

Write what happens next.

_____

_____

_____

Writing

The Y's of

Why do people write?

I want to **explain** how something works.

I want to **persuade**, or share my opinion.

I want to **narrate**, or tell a story.

I want to **inform**, or tell facts.

inform   explain   narrate   persuade

Read what Yin wrote.

Do you want to cook a yam?

Scrub the yam until it is clean.

Wrap the yam in foil.

Put the yam into a hot oven. Wait one hour!

Why did Yin write this? He wants to _____.

Read what Yvette wrote.

Yams are the best dish at Thanksgiving.

They are better than mashed potatoes!

You can melt marshmallows on them.

Try them!

Why did Yvette write this? She wants to _____.

Writing

My grandma talks funny.

Her y's sounds like j's.

When she says yellow, it sounds like jello!

Once she asked me to bring her yam.

I brought her jam.

She stamped her feet. "Yam! yam!"

I heard, "Jam! jam!"

I thought about it.

The next day, I brought her a bag with…

"Yam!" she cried. She cooked it. We ate it. We laughed.

Why did Yale write this? He wants to _____.

Read what Ynez wrote.

A yam is an orange vegetable.

Some are the size of a small potato.

Others are as big as a watermelon. (Or bigger!)

A yam has a lot of vitamins.

Why did Ynez write this? She wants to _____.

Yamakake is a Japanese dish.
Guess what's in it?

Tell It!

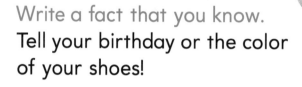

Write a fact that you know. Tell your birthday or the color of your shoes!

Did you know that

_____

_____?

Explain how to do something. **Need an idea?** Explain how to make a sandwich.

Here is how to _____

_____

_____ .

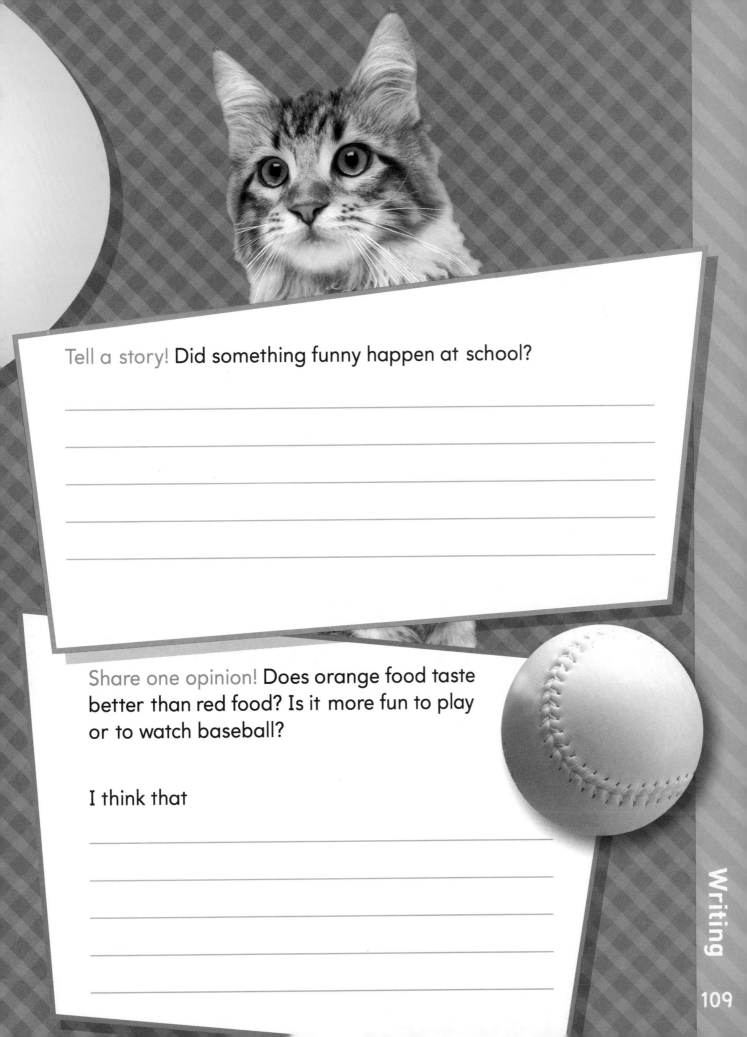

Tell a story! Did something funny happen at school?

_____

_____

_____

_____

_____

Share one opinion! Does orange food taste better than red food? Is it more fun to play or to watch baseball?

I think that

_____

_____

_____

_____

Caption Contest

A **caption** tells about a picture.
Write a caption for each.

Write a caption about *me*!

Family Portrait

You can paint a picture with words!
Describe your family using words.

The people in my family are

_____
_____
_____
_____
_____

On the weekends, we like to

_____
_____
_____
_____

Our favorite thing to cook is

_____
_____
_____
_____
_____

Forget Me Not

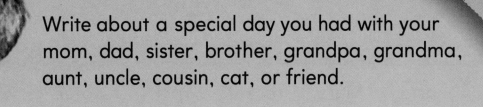

Write about a special day you had with your mom, dad, sister, brother, grandpa, grandma, aunt, uncle, cousin, cat, or friend.

One day

Then

Finally

Rover Red Rover

Finish the sentences about the Mars rover.

| arm | Mars | rocket | rocks | water | wheels |

The rover landed on planet _____.

A _____ helped get it there.

The planet Mars is covered in red _____.

The rover has big _____ to help it move over the rocks.

The rover uses its _____ to collect rocks.

The rover has a job. It is looking for signs of _____.

A rover is a robot scientist! Rover names are Spirit, Opportunity, and Curiosity.

The Curiosity rover went to Mars in 2012. It collects rock samples. It will stay on Mars forever!

Write a note to the Curiosity rover. Ask it a question about Mars.

Dear Curiosity,

_____

_____

_____

NASA/JPL/Cornell University

I Think...

Everyone has an opinion! Opinions are things you think or believe. What do you think? Write it below.

I think chewing gum should be against the law.

I think dogs are the best pets.

I think summer is more fun than winter.

I think

Do you want someone to share your opinion?

Tell them why you think it!

I think

One reason is

Another reason is

I think snails are good pets. One reason is that they're quiet. Another reason is that they don't eat too much. But that's just my opinion.

Away We Go!

The Santana family is having a reunion. There are lots of ways to get there! Complete the sentences.

nouns

bike   boat   bus   plane

verbs

drives   flies   rides   sails

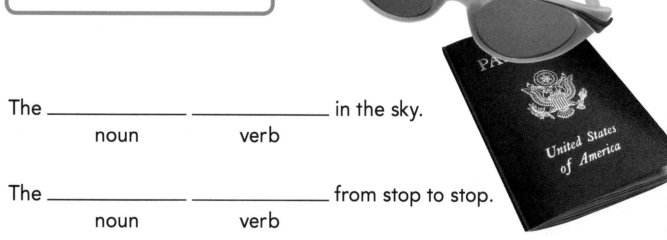

The _____ _____ in the sky.
　　　noun　　　　　verb

The _____ _____ from stop to stop.
　　　noun　　　　　verb

The _____ _____ on the ocean.
　　　noun　　　　　verb

The _____ _____ down the street.
　　　noun　　　　　verb

How did each person get there? Solve it!
Then write a sentence.

Rafael lives only three blocks away.

Rafael

Maja lives across the ocean. But she is afraid to fly!

Tía lives far away. She gets seasick.

Adela is coming! But she wants to sightsee along the way.

Animals Amok!

What are the animals doing?

nouns: bat   cheetah   crocodile   hyena   monkey

verbs: eats   hangs   laughs   runs   swims

The _____ _____ upside down.
      noun   verb

The _____ _____ fast.
      noun   verb

The _____ _____ fruit.
      noun   verb

The _____ _____. What is so funny?
      noun   verb

The _____ _____ in the river.
      noun   verb

Draw an animal doing something.
Write one sentence to tell what it
is doing.

The _____

There It Goes!

Everyone and everything is on the go! What do you see? Write a sentence. Start it with *There goes a...*

firetruck

There goes a
_____.

penguin

_____.

train

_____.

_____.

baby

chicken

_____.

Dragon and Unicorn Are Best Friends!

Write sentences to describe dragon and unicorn. Use a **verb**, **adjective**, and **noun**!

VERBS: breathes   drinks   eats   makes

ADJECTIVES: bright   hot   pretty   sparkly

NOUNS: fire   food   rainbows   sunshine

Unicorn drinks sparkly sunshine.

Dragon

Unicorn

Big BAD Rolf!

Rolf is a wolf. Everyone thinks
he is big and bad. He thinks he is nice and friendly!
Use the words to complete each sentence.

| furry | happy | juicy | scary | sharp | shy |

Rolf is a ＿＿＿＿＿＿ wolf.

Don't scream! He doesn't want to be ＿＿＿＿＿＿.

He has ＿＿＿＿＿＿teeth.

He uses his teeth to eat ＿＿＿＿＿＿ apples.

Sometimes he feels quiet

and ＿＿＿＿＿＿

around new people.

Being a friend makes Rolf

a ＿＿＿＿＿＿ wolf.

1000

Some people say a picture is worth a thousand words. **Finish the picture.**

Words

That's an interesting drawing! **Write a short story about it.** Use nouns, verbs, and adjectives.

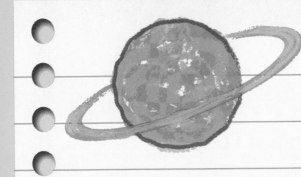

Tell your story to someone!

help This sentince

Willa wrote a letter to Edith. Look for mistakes.
Circle them.

Did she spell everything right?

Did she punctuate her sentences?

Did she use capital letters where they belong?

Dear Dr edith,

thank yuo for taking care of fluffy.

She feles much better

you are a grate doctor!

Your friend,
Willa

Addition
and
Subtraction

Hop, Skip, JUMP

Jump ahead by the number shown. **Write the number the animal lands on.**

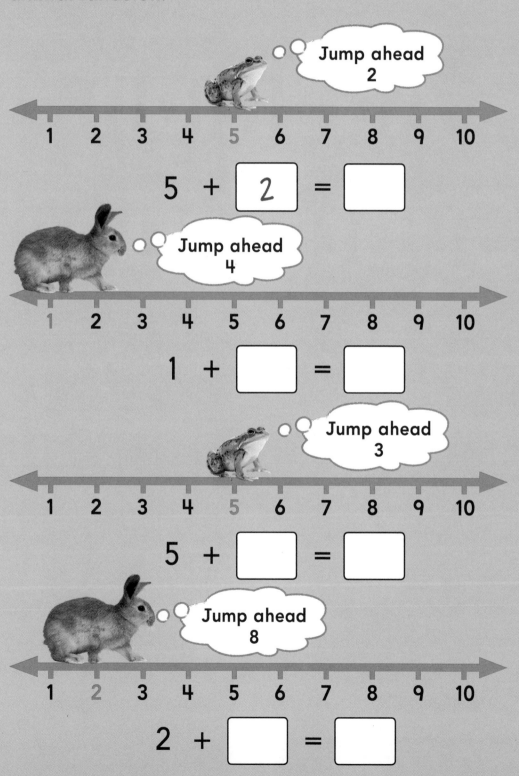

Jump ahead
2

1 2 3 4 5 6 7 8 9 10

5 + 2 = ☐

Jump ahead
4

1 2 3 4 5 6 7 8 9 10

1 + ☐ = ☐

Jump ahead
3

1 2 3 4 5 6 7 8 9 10

5 + ☐ = ☐

Jump ahead
8

1 2 3 4 5 6 7 8 9 10

2 + ☐ = ☐

Beach Treasure

Count how many treasures the Garcia sisters collected at the beach. **Write the number** in the box below. **Write the total number** in the last box.

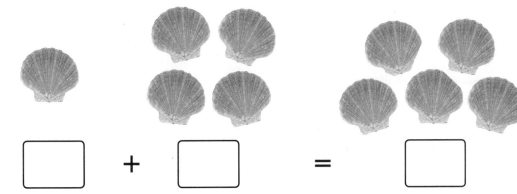

$$\boxed{} + \boxed{} = \boxed{}$$

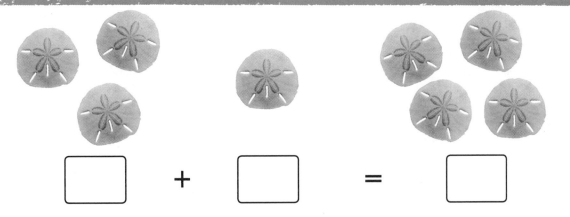

$$\boxed{} + \boxed{} = \boxed{}$$

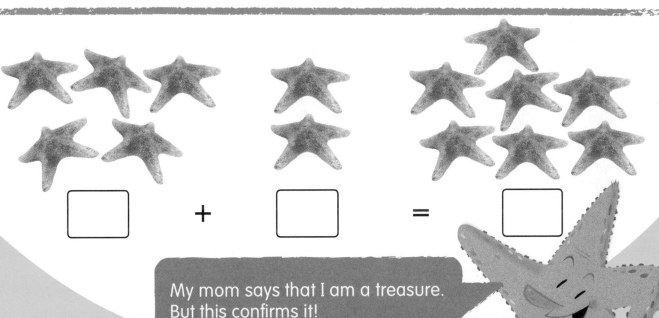

$$\boxed{} + \boxed{} = \boxed{}$$

My mom says that I am a treasure. But this confirms it!

Clean Your Room!

Jack cleaned his room. Count the toys he found. Write the numbers in the boxes. Write the sum in the last box.

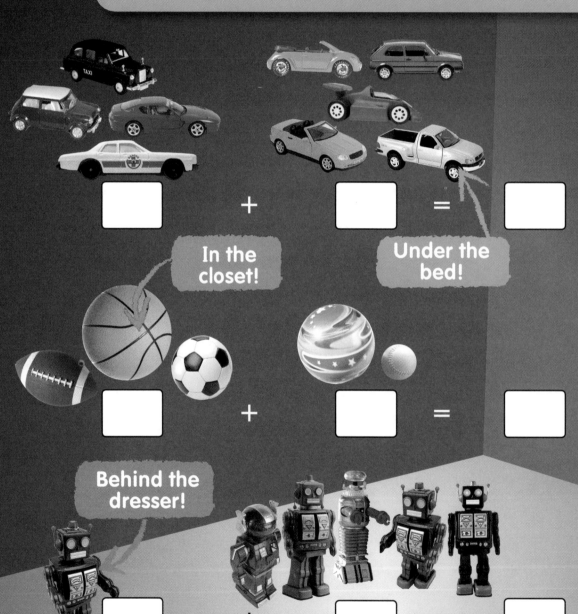

[ ] + [ ] = [ ]

In the closet!

Under the bed!

[ ] + [ ] = [ ]

Behind the dresser!

[ ] + [ ] = [ ]

That's a lot of toys! If Jack has 20 toys, he promises to give me one. How many toys does Jack have in all?

Fruity Fun

Draw fruit in the bowls to match the numbers. Then write the sum in the box.

$1 + 2 = \boxed{3}$

$4 + 1 = \boxed{}$

$1 + 8 = \boxed{}$

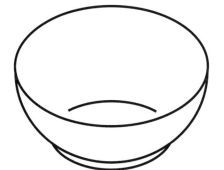

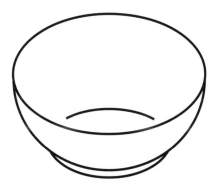

$3 + 4 = \boxed{}$

My favorite fruit is a star fruit. The fancy name for star fruit is Carambola! My fancy name is Cosmo.

Mattress Mountain

Princess Elena likes to sleep on a lot of mattresses. Write the number of mattresses in each row. Then write the sum in the bottom box.

Leaning Book Tower!

Asher sorts his books into piles. Write the number of books in each pile. Then write the sum in the bottom box. Does he have more dinosaur books or cookbooks?

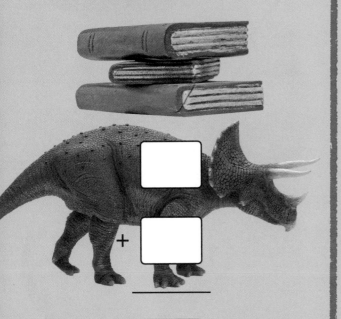

dinosaur books

cookbooks

Birthday Surprise!

The baker needs help putting candles on the right cakes. **Add the candles** in each group. Then **draw a line** to the cake with the matching number.

9

7

6

10

My Aunt Cora is a sea star. It's her birthday! She is 23 years old. Counting to 23 is easy. Eating birthday cake underwater is not.

Tropical ADVENTURE!

Dash and Anna visit a tropical rainforest.
They see amazing things!

Dash sees 2 red parrots.

Anna sees 3 green parrots.

How many parrots are there?

☐ parrots

Dash sees 4 coconut trees.

Anna sees 1 pineapple tree.

How many trees are there?

☐ trees

Dash sees 6 crawling bugs.

Anna sees 2 flying bugs.

How many bugs are there?

☐ bugs

Addition and Subtraction

137

Treasure TROVE

Gus found a total of 10 shiny coins. 4 coins are gold.
The rest are silver. How many **silver coins** did Gus find?

4	

10

Gus found a total of 9 colorful gems. He found 3 rubies
under a rock. He found some green emeralds under a tree.
How many **green emeralds** did Gus find?

3	

9

LUCKY 7!

7 is a lucky number! Draw more ribbons so each group has 7. Write the number of ribbons you drew.

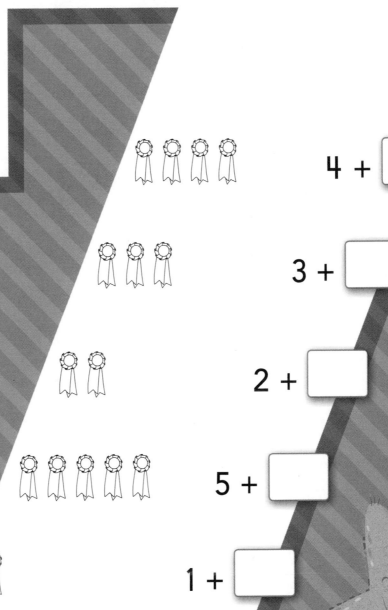

4 + ▢

3 + ▢

2 + ▢

5 + ▢

1 + ▢

Lucky sea star numbers are 5, 10, 20, and 40. Can you guess why? I'll give you a hint! My lucky number is 5.

Top

Igor the Magician has 5 black hats and 5 white hats. He has 10 hats altogether!

$$5 + 5 = 10$$

Make some magic!

Color **some** of the hats blue. Color **the rest** of the hats yellow. Write how many hats are blue. Write how many are yellow.

☐ + ☐ = 10

Ten

Color **some** of the hats red. Color **the rest** of the hats blue. Then write how many hats are red. Write how many hats are blue.

$$\boxed{} + \boxed{} = 10$$

Color **some** of the hats yellow. Color **the rest** of the hats red. Then write how many hats are yellow. Write how many hats are red.

$$\boxed{} + \boxed{} = 10$$

If you don't have crayons, write a letter on the hat instead! **B** for blue, **Y** for yellow, and **R** for red. Did you know that sea stars come in these colors?

Double Fun Numbers!

Double the number. Double the fun!
Add twin numbers to get your sum!

$$\begin{array}{r} 3 \\ +3 \\ \hline \end{array}$$ $$\begin{array}{r} 4 \\ +4 \\ \hline \end{array}$$ $$\begin{array}{r} 5 \\ +5 \\ \hline \end{array}$$ $$\begin{array}{r} 6 \\ +6 \\ \hline \end{array}$$ $$\begin{array}{r} 7 \\ +7 \\ \hline \end{array}$$

$$\begin{array}{r} 8 \\ +8 \\ \hline \end{array}$$ $$\begin{array}{r} 9 \\ +9 \\ \hline \end{array}$$ $$\begin{array}{r} 10 \\ +10 \\ \hline \end{array}$$

Making Cents

Add the coins together. Then match the sum to the correct piggy bank.

3¢

20¢

25¢

10¢

15¢

penny	=	1 cent	=	1¢
nickel	=	5 cents	=	5¢
dime	=	10 cents	=	10¢
quarter	=	25 cents	=	25¢

Back to School

Write how many fish are in each group. Add the numbers.
Write the sum in the last box.

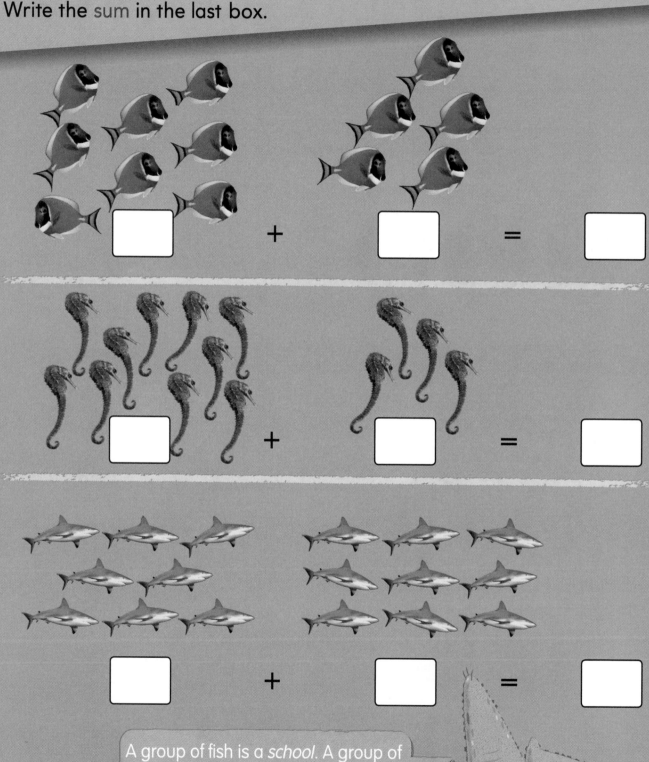

□ + □ = □

□ + □ = □

□ + □ = □

A group of fish is a *school*. A group of
seahorses is a *herd*. And a group of
sharks is a *problem*. No, really! *SWIM!*

Beautiful Broccoli

Sara is planting a broccoli garden. How many plants will she grow? Count each group of seeds. Write the number of seeds in each group. Write the sum in the last box.

[ ] + [ ] = [ ]

[ ] + [ ] = [ ]

[ ] + [ ] = [ ]

Zzz!

Adam is sleepy. He's catching some Zzz's! But how many? **Add the numbers. Write the sum** in each box.

$1 + 3 + 5 = \boxed{}$ Z's

$2 + 8 + 3 = \boxed{}$ Z's

$5 + 9 + 1 = \boxed{}$ Z's

$4 + 4 + 6 = \boxed{}$ Z's

$3 + 2 + 9 = \boxed{}$ Z's

$7 + 2 + 3 = \boxed{}$ Z's

$6 + 2 + 2 = \boxed{}$ Z's

The Wheel of Fun!

There are three pairs of cars on the Ferris wheel. Yellow, blue, and red. A number is missing in each pair! Fill it in. The numbers in each pair must add up to the number in the middle!

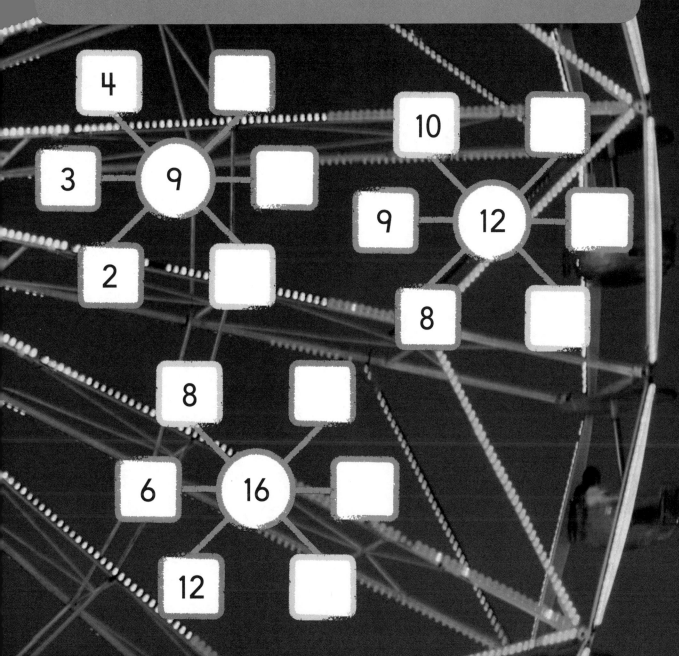

147

What's the

Add the numbers. **Write the sum on the cone!**

8
+ 2
◯

7
+ 10
◯

3
+ 2
◯

10
+ 10
◯

11
+ 4
◯

5
+ 3
◯

4
+ 8
◯

2
+ 7
◯

Scp?

6
+ 5
◯

5
+ 8
◯

4
+ 7
◯

9
+ 7
◯

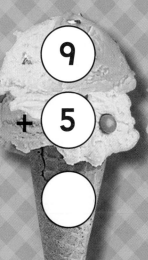

9
+ 5
◯

1
+ 9
◯

3
+ 4
◯

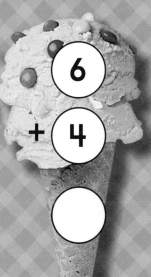

6
+ 4
◯

What's your favorite number flavor?

JUMP Back Jack

Jack the rabbit can only jump backward! **Jump back** by the number shown. Write the number he lands on.

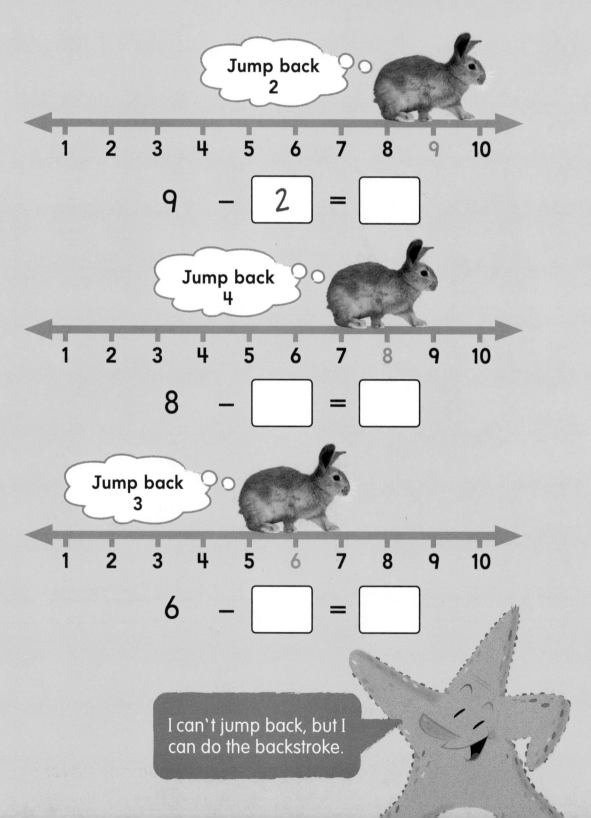

Jump back
2

1 2 3 4 5 6 7 8 9 10

9 – 2 = ☐

Jump back
4

1 2 3 4 5 6 7 8 9 10

8 – ☐ = ☐

Jump back
3

1 2 3 4 5 6 7 8 9 10

6 – ☐ = ☐

I can't jump back, but I can do the backstroke.

Bye-bye, Birdie!

It's time for the baby birds to leave the nest!

 − =

 − =

 −   =

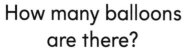

Pop! Pop! Pop!

Poppy the porcupine loves to pop balloons!

How many balloons are there?	How many does Poppy pop?	How many balloons are left?

Pop!

☐ – ☐ = ☐

Pop!
Pop! Pop!

☐ – ☐ = ☐

Pop! Pop!
Pop! Pop!

☐ – ☐ = ☐

My cousin Gareth is prickly. He's a sea urchin.
People call him the "hedgehog of the sea."
But I think he looks like the porcupine of the sea.

Ready, Set, Throw!

Corey throws a ball at a stack of cans. Some cans are still standing. How many did she knock over?

Cookie Thief!

Yikes! Someone stole a cookie at Grandma Jane's house! **Count the cookies. How many are left? How many are missing?**

$-$

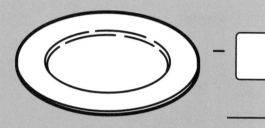

$-$

$-$

$-$

The MISSING Marbles

Jamal lost his marbles!
Draw an X over lost marbles.
How many of each color are left?

Jamal had 6 red marbles. He lost 3.

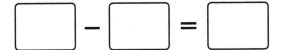

[ ] are left.

[ ] – [ ] = [ ]

Jamal had 7 blue marbles. He lost 2.

[ ] are left.

[ ] – [ ] = [ ]

Jamal had 9 green marbles. He lost 4.

[ ] are left.

[ ] – [ ] = [ ]

Traffic JAM!

Six cars are stuck in traffic.
Three cars go home.
How many cars are left?

[ ] − [ ] = [ ]

Seven birds fly over the city.
Five fly away.
How many birds are left?

[ ] − [ ] = [ ]

Snow Day!

Subtract the numbers. Write the difference on the bottom snowball!

10

− 5

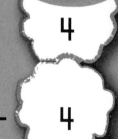

4

− 4

8

− 4

9

− 8

12

− 2

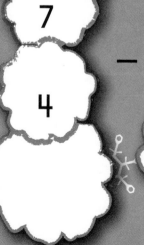

7

− 4

10

− 3

7

− 6

8
− 2

6
− 5

5
− 3

7
− 1

6
− 3

10
− 7

9
− 5

6
− 4

Hungry Hedgehog!

Hillary the hedgehog is hungry for bugs!
Draw an X over the bugs she eats.
How many are left?

Hillary finds 8 beetles.
She eats 6.

[ ] are left.

[ ] − [ ] = [ ]

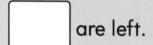

Hillary finds 5 worms.
She eats 4.

[ ] is left.

[ ] − [ ] = [ ]

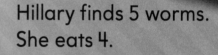
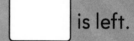

Hillary finds 8 snails.
She eats 5.

[ ] are left.

[ ] − [ ] = [ ]

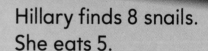
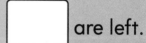
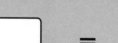

Math Facts

Number Family

Numbers have families too. And this number family likes to rock! **Add or subtract to make a math fact family.**

2 + 1 = ☐   1 + 2 = ☐

3 − 2 = ☐   3 − 1 = ☐

3 + 2 = ☐   2 + 3 = ☐

5 − 2 = ☐   5 − 3 = ☐

2 + ☐ = ☐   ☐ + 2 = ☐

☐ − 2 = ☐   4 − ☐ = ☐

Fact families are number sentences that use the same three numbers.

Fuzzy Family

The Gibson family wants to adopt a pet! Look at the fuzzy families. Add or subtract to make a fuzzy fact family.

$$6 + 3 = 9$$
$$3 + 6 = 9$$
$$9 - 6 = 3$$

1. $\boxed{7} + \boxed{5} = \boxed{12}$

$\boxed{} - \boxed{} = \boxed{}$

$\boxed{} + \boxed{} = \boxed{}$

2. $\boxed{} + \boxed{} = \boxed{}$

$\boxed{} - \boxed{} = \boxed{}$

$\boxed{11} - \boxed{6} = \boxed{5}$

QUACK!
HONK!
Peep!

Help the mother birds find their eggs. **Fill in the numbers on each egg. Then draw a line to the correct bird.**

1 2 + [ ] = 5
   5 – 2 = [ ]

2 6 + [ ] = 12
   12 – 6 = [ ]

3 3 + [ ] = 7
   7 – 3 = [ ]

4 4 + [ ] = 9
   9 – 4 = [ ]

5

3

4

6

TOY SWAP!

Jose and his friends swap toys. Add or subtract to show how many toys Jose takes home. **Write a + or – sign in the box.**

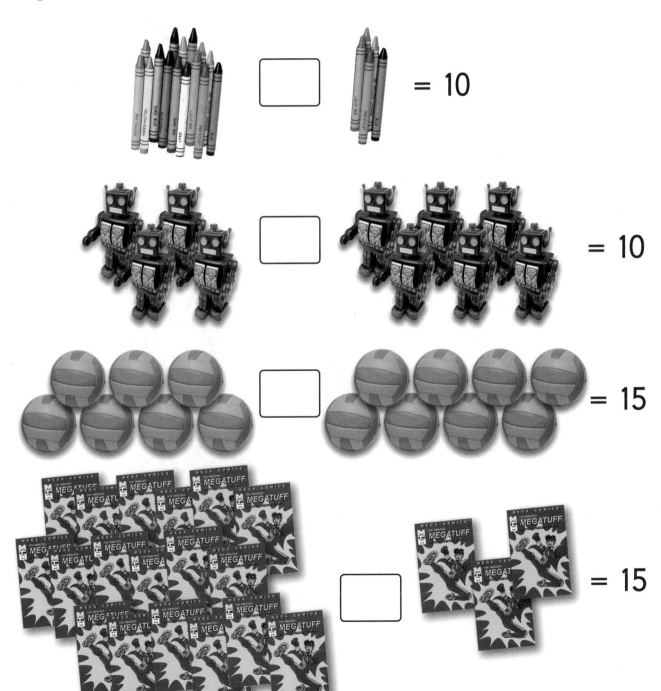

= 10

= 10

= 15

= 15

CODE CRUNCHER!

Count before you crunch! **Follow the code to count back.**

 means count back 1.

 means count back 2.

 means count back 3.

10   9

9

8

6

12

7

5

11

Just the Facts, Math

The math detective will ask the questions here. **Do you have answers?**

$$5 \\ +6$$ □

$$11 \\ -7$$ □

$$4 \\ +8$$ □

$$3 \\ +3$$ □

$$17 \\ -15$$ □

$$9 \\ -1$$ □

The detective wants more facts. **Choose 3 numbers to make a subtraction fact.** Then add to check your fact.

5, 8, 12, 7

___ − ___ = ___

___ + ___ = ___

16, 5, 7, 9

___ − ___ = ___

___ + ___ = ___

11, 6, 13, 5

___ − ___ = ___

___ + ___ = ___

CRAFTY Chloe

Chloe loves to make presents for her friends. Write a number sentence to describe each craft project. **Write a + or – sign in the circle.**

Chloe makes a bracelet with 21 beads. 3 beads fall off. How many beads are left?

_____ ◯ _____ = _____ beads

Chloe glues 15 shells onto a picture frame. *Not enough!* She adds 6 more shells. How many shells are on the frame?

_____ ◯ _____ = _____ shells

Chloe makes a caterpillar with 18 pom-poms. Her cat steals 9 pom-poms. How many pom-poms are left?

_____ ◯ _____ = _____ pom-poms

Chloe makes a model of the White House with 100 popsicle sticks. She sends it the President. He adds 20 popsicle sticks. How many sticks are on the model?

_____ ◯ _____ = _____ popsicle sticks

Number
and
Operations

H OP IT UP!

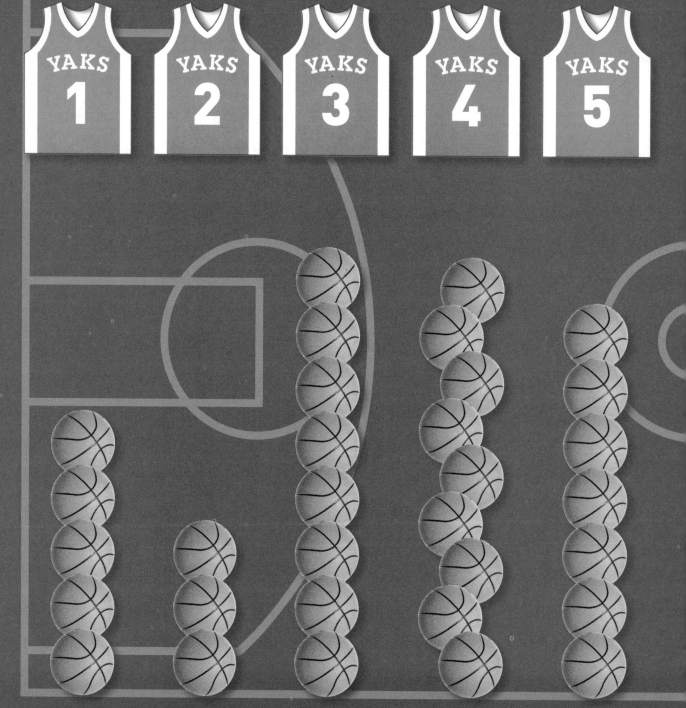

Go Yaks! The mighty Yaks won their first basketball game.
Match the number of basketballs **to a jersey.**

TWO BY TWO!

It's a wild parade! Count the animals.
Write the number in the box.

Say the numbers out loud.
You're counting by 2s!

Cheese!

Smile! Paolo is having a cheese party. Count the number of holes in each cheese. Write the number in the box.

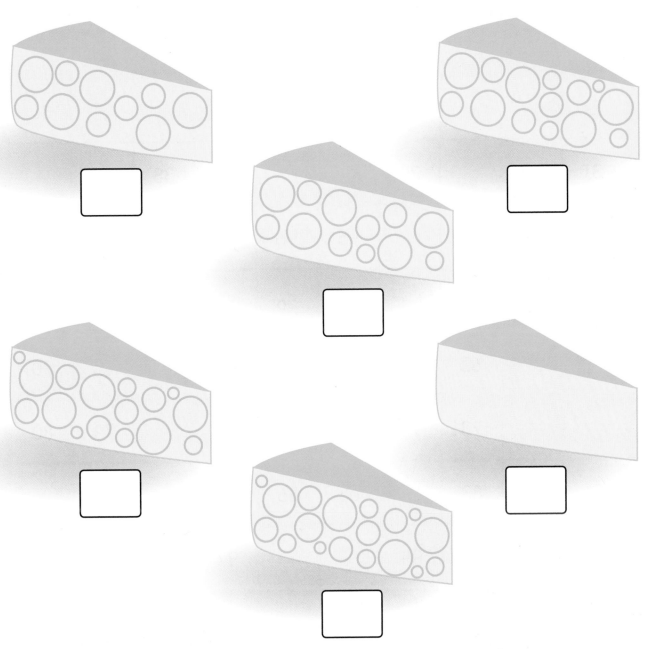

Skip count to figure out how many holes should be in the last cheese. Write the number in the box. Then draw them.

Penny's PENNIES

Penny's pocket is full of pennies. Help her count them! **Fill in the missing numbers.**

1	2			5	6		8		10
11	12				16	17			20
21				25		27			30
31	32		34	35		37	38		
	42			45	46	47			50
51	52				56	57		59	
61		63		65	66		68		70
		73	74		76			79	80
81	82	83	84	85	86				
91		93	94			97	98		100

Penny has a lucky penny. **Which one is it?**
Count by 2s seven times! The lucky penny is number ☐ !

Five Cents!

It's a hot day! Jamie and Madge sell lemonade for 5 cents a cup. **Write the missing numbers in the yellow boxes.**

1	2	3	4		6	7	8	9	
11	12	13	14		16	17	18	19	
21	22	23	24		26	27	28	29	
31	32	33	34		36	37	38	39	
41	42	43	44		46	47	48	49	
51	52	53	54		56	57	58	59	
61	62	63	64		66	67	68	69	
71	72	73	74		76	77	78	79	
81	82	83	84		86	87	88	89	
91	92	93	94		96	97	98	99	

Say the numbers in the yellow boxes out loud! You're counting by 5s.

5 Little Piggies

These little piggies love nickels! Count by 5s to match the nickels to the piggy bank.

5¢

20¢

25¢

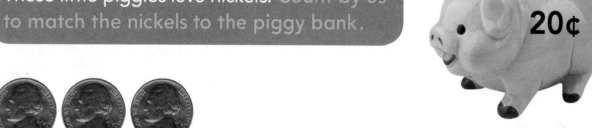

10¢

15¢

30¢

Tommy Takes Ten

Tommy took all the 10s in this chart!
Fill them back in.

1	2	3	4	5	6	7	8	9	
11	12	13	14	15	16	17	18	19	
21	22	23	24	25	26	27	28	29	
31	32	33	34	35	36	37	38	39	
41	42	43	44	45	46	47	48	49	
51	52	53	54	55	56	57	58	59	
61	62	63	64	65	66	67	68	69	
71	72	73	74	75	76	77	78	79	
81	82	83	84	85	86	87	88	89	
91	92	93	94	95	96	97	98	99	
101	102	103	104	105	106	107	108	109	
111	112	113	114	115	116	117	118	119	

I SPY IN SPACE!

Astronauts Sofie and Ben play "I spy."
How many of each thing do they spy?

moons

stars

planets

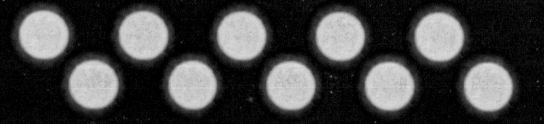

suns

asteroids

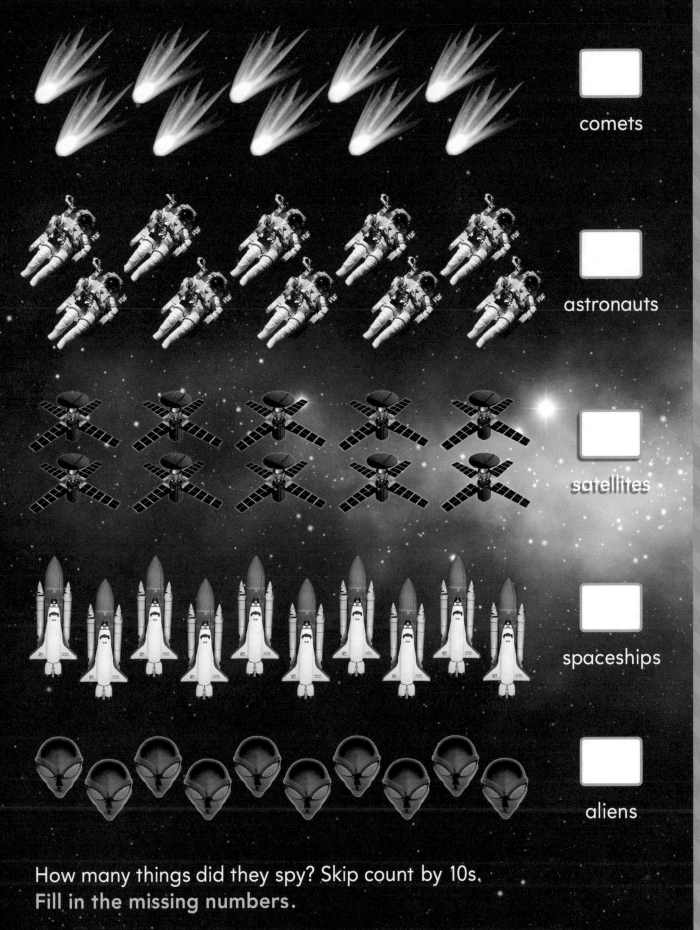

comets

astronauts

satellites

spaceships

aliens

How many things did they spy? Skip count by 10s.
Fill in the missing numbers.

10, ____, 30, ____, ____, 60, ____, ____, ____, 100

Number and Operations

MORE or LESS!

Pip always has five less. Kip always has five more! **Skip count by 5s to fill in the blanks.**

5 less		5 more
	10	
	25	
	40	
	5	
		85
55		

Lou always has ten less. Sue always has ten more! **Skip count by 10s to fill in the blanks.**

10 less		10 more
	17	
	33	
60		
18		
		42
		59

Cuckoo Catastrophe!

The cuckoo clock shop has a problem.
Some numbers have fallen off the clocks!
Write the missing numbers on the clocks.

The missing numbers on the first clock are odd. The
missing numbers on the second clock are even. **Say the
numbers.** You'll be counting by **odd** or by **even** numbers!

184

ODD Soup

Talia and Emil make soup. Count how many of each ingredient they need. **Write the number in the box. Circle if each number is odd or even.**

[ ] odd or even

[ ] odd or even

[ ] odd or even

[ ] odd or even

[ ] odd or even

[ ] odd or even

Number and Operations

185

Cheddar Towers

CHEESY!

Tilly builds towers out of cheese cubes. Each tower has ten cubes. How many groups of ten do you see? **Write the number below.**

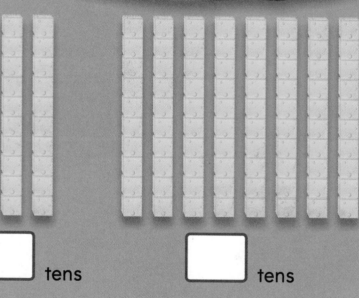

[ ] tens

[ ] tens

[ ] tens

[ ] tens

[ ] tens

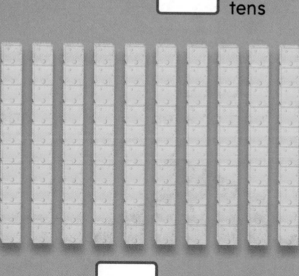

[ ] tens

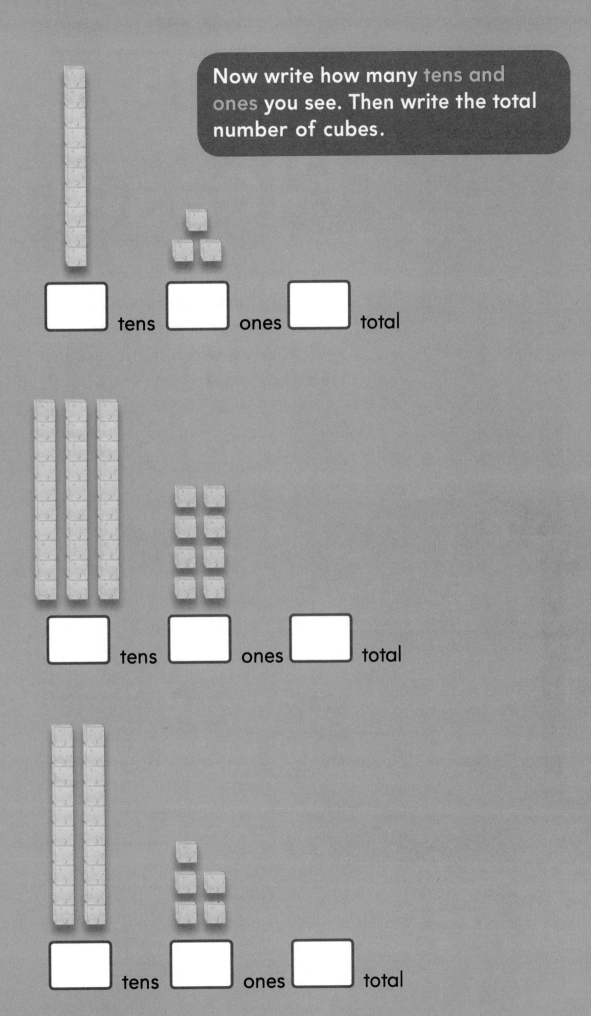

[ ] tens [ ] ones [ ] total

[ ] tens [ ] ones [ ] total

[ ] tens [ ] ones [ ] total

Number and Operations

187

Places, Please!

Every number has its place. Look at these numbers. Write which number is in the **tens** place. Write which number is in the **ones** place.

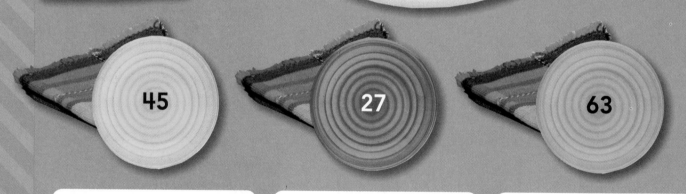

45 **27** **63**

__4__ tens __5__ ones   ____ tens ____ ones   ____ tens ____ ones

18 **51** **39**

____ tens ____ ones   ____ tens ____ ones   ____ tens ____ ones

10 Little Piggies

These little piggies love dimes! **Count by 10s** to match the dimes to the piggy bank.

Hamster Safari

Henry goes on a wild hamster safari. How many hamsters does he see?

Write the number of **tens** in the first box. Write the number of **ones** in the second box. **Then write the total.**

☐ tens + ☐ ones = ◯ total

☐ tens + ☐ ones = ◯ total

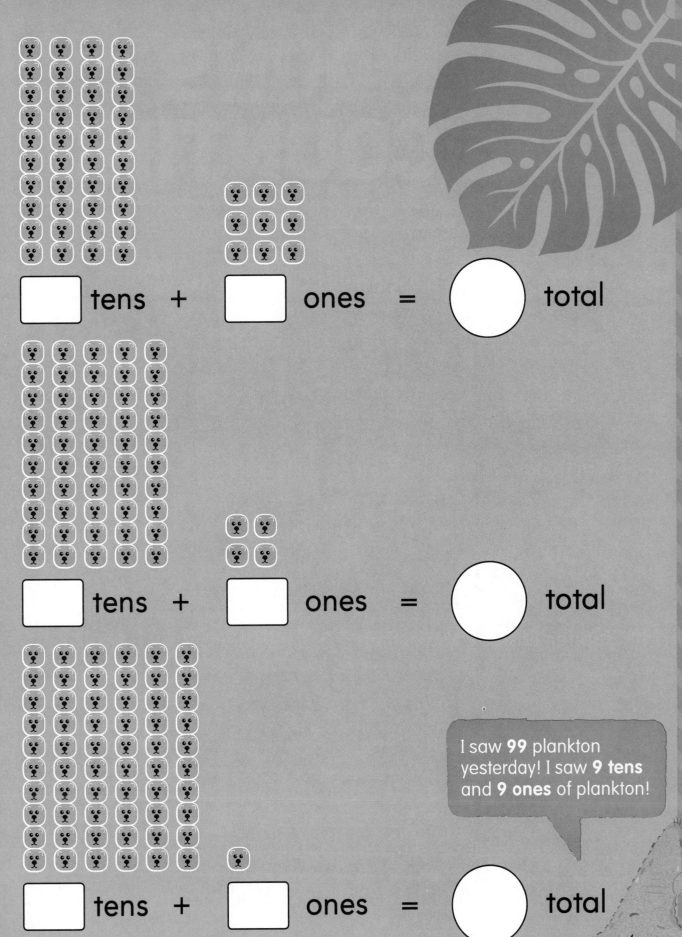

[ ] tens + [ ] ones = ( ) total

[ ] tens + [ ] ones = ( ) total

I saw **99** plankton yesterday! I saw **9 tens** and **9 ones** of plankton!

[ ] tens + [ ] ones = ( ) total

Many MOONS and COUNTING!

Some planets have more moons than others. Does the first planet in each pair have more than or less than the other planet? **Circle the answer.**

1

2

Earth has   more than   less than   Mars

50

53

Jupiter has   more than   less than   Saturn

27

13

Uranus has   more than   less than   Neptune

There are 146 "known" moons. Astronomers keep looking for more! Moons can have names like Rhea, Juliet, and Thelxinoe! Earth's moon is called Earth's Moon.

Gary's Twigs

Gary the rhino eats twigs. Count the twigs in each group. **Write a < or > symbol to show which group has more twigs.**

[<]

[ ]

[ ]

[ ]

The < symbol means *is less than*. 2 arms < 5 arms.
The > symbol means *is greater than*. 5 arms > 2 arms.
It is pretty great to have 5 arms!

Busting the Banks!

Cap		Liz

   **>**

  ☐

   ☐

  ☐

Who has more money? Cap or Liz? **Write a**
< or > symbol to show who has more money.

Cap   Liz

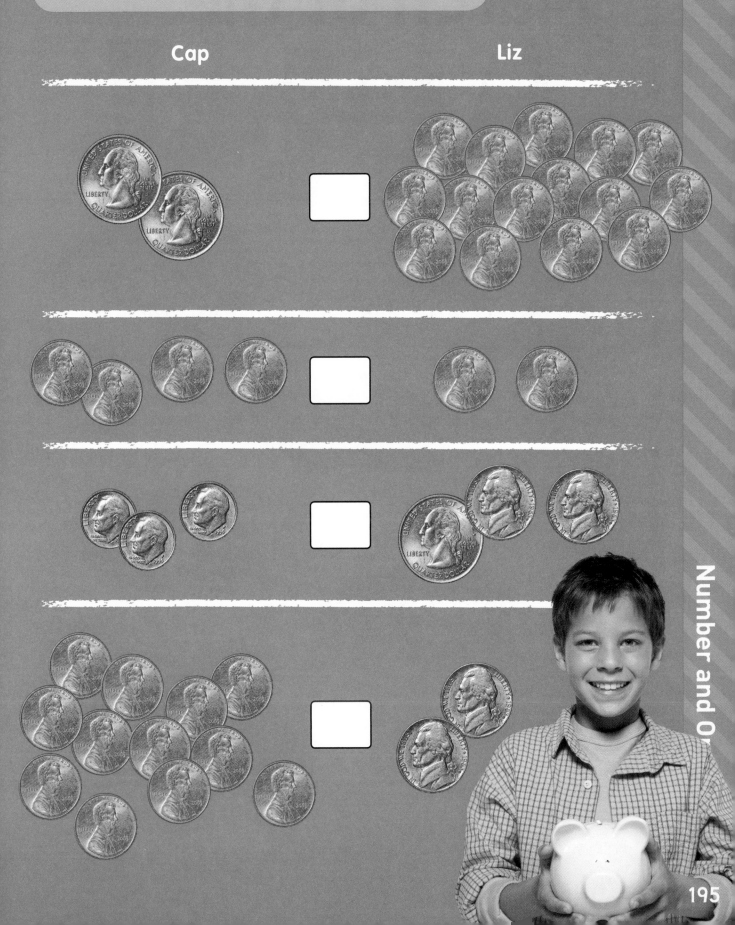

Number and O

March of the Ants!

4 ones + 4 ones

4 tens + 2 tens

3 ones + 2 ones

3 tens + 5 tens

5 ones + 1 one

2 tens + 5 tens

Help the ants carry each leaf home. Draw a line from the leaf to its sum. Then draw a line from the sum to its anthill.

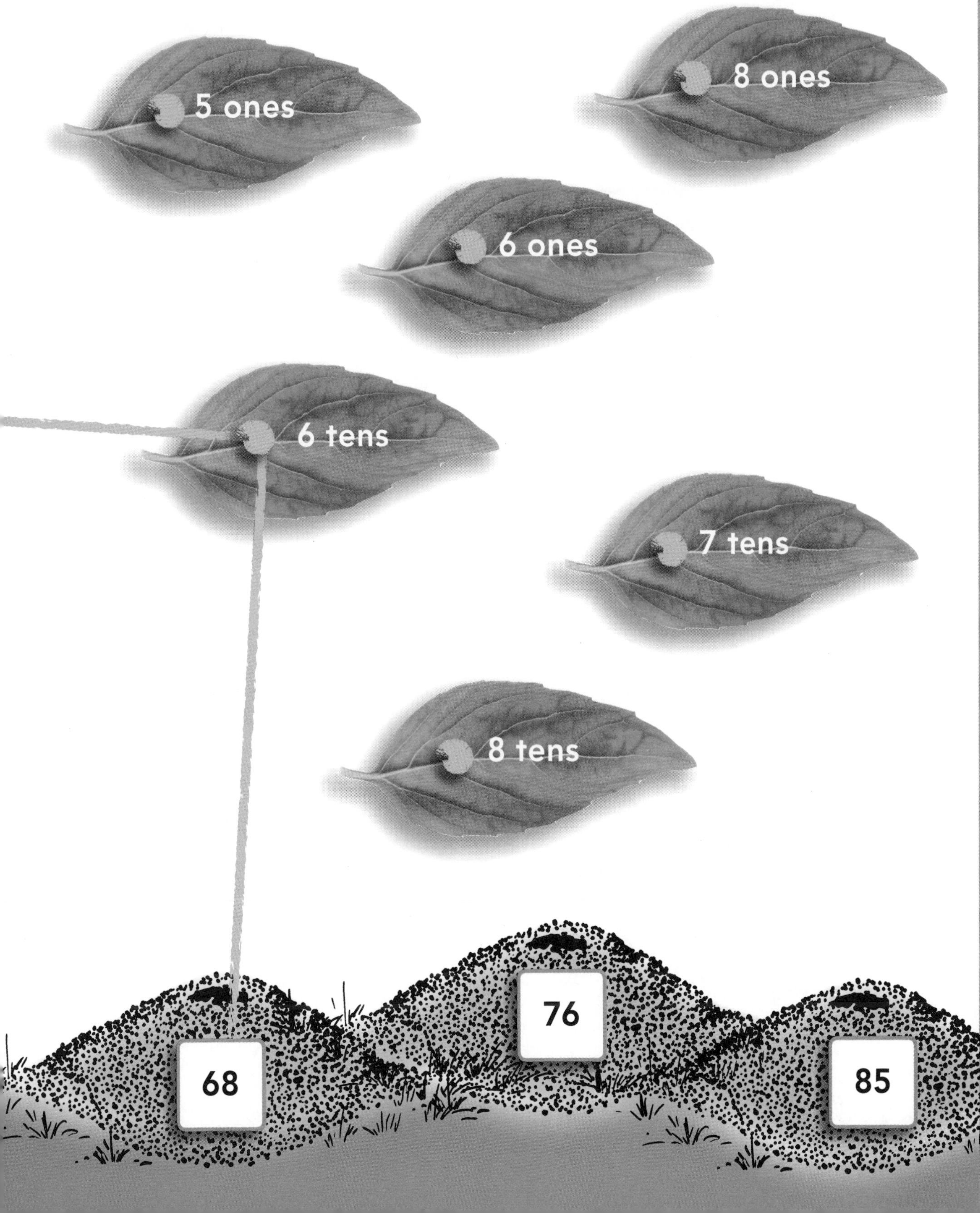

5 ones

8 ones

6 ones

6 tens

7 tens

8 tens

76

68

85

Guess My

43 is 10 less than my number.

100 is 10 more than my number.

63 is 10 more than my number.

75 is 10 more than my number.

Number!

55 is 10
less than
my number.

[ ]

My number
is 10 less
than 10.

[ ]

71 is 10
less than
my number.

[ ]

My number
is 10 more
than 88.

[ ]

GROSS Estimates

Guess, or **estimate**, how many eyeballs are in each jar.
Then **count** the actual number. Did you guess correctly?

		I estimate	I count
1		_____ s	_____ s
2		_____ s	_____ s
3		_____ s	_____ s
4		_____ s	_____ s

Measurement
and
Data

NatureWalk

June found some animals!
Use the ruler to measure them.
How many inches is each animal?

inches

It is about _____ inches.

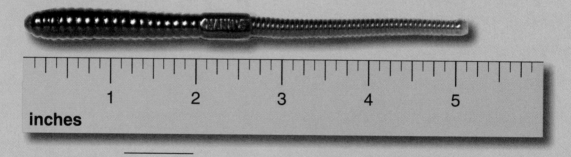

inches

It is about _____ inches.

inches

It is about _____ inches.

Lost Wand! BIG Reward!

Magic Maxine lost her wand! **Help her describe it.**

My wand is about _____  high.

My wand is about _____ high.

My wand is **longer than a pencil**.
It is the **same length as a drinking straw**.
Draw the wand and the straw.

pencil	
wand	
straw	

TALLY-HO!

The sheep dog lost her sheep!
They are playing with the pigs.
Count the sheep and pigs.
Make a tally mark for each one.
Then count the tally marks.
Write the total.

Animals		Total
sheep dog	/	1
sheep		
pigs		

Class PET

Mr. Parker's class voted for a class pet. Look at the picture graph. **Answer the questions.**

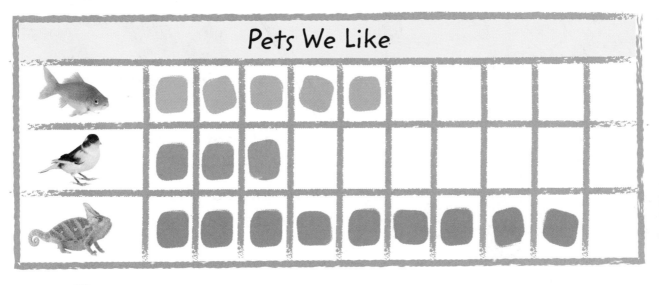

Pets We Like

Each  stands for 1 kid.

How many kids want a fish? _____

How many kids want a bird? _____

How many kids want a lizard? _____

The Great Race

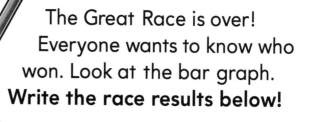

The Great Race is over! Everyone wants to know who won. Look at the bar graph. **Write the race results below!**

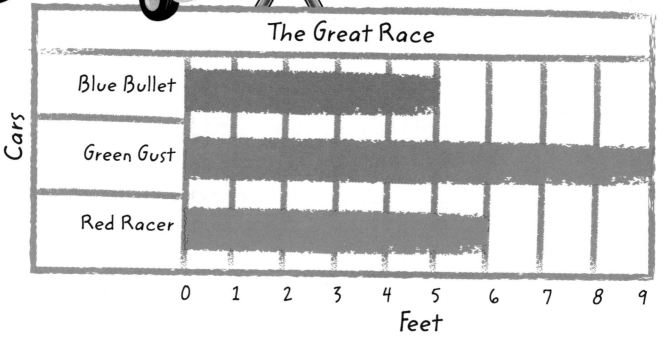

Green Gust beat Red Racer by _____ feet!

Blue Bullet came in last. It was _____ feet behind Green Gust!

If Green Gust traveled 4 fewer feet, which car would win the race? _____

206

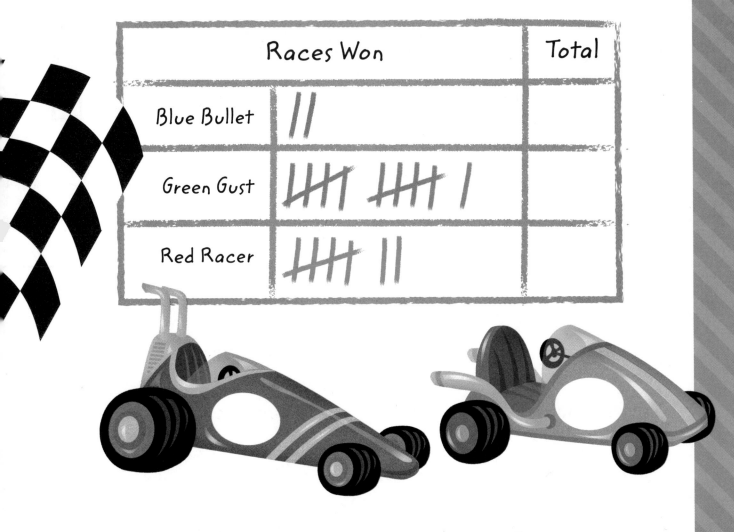

Races Won		Total
Blue Bullet	||	
Green Gust	₩₩ ₩₩ |	
Red Racer	₩₩ ||	

Is **Green Gust** the fastest car on the block? The tally chart shows how many races each car won.

Which car color won 11 races? _____

Which car color won 4 fewer times than **Green Gust**?
_____

Which car color won 2 races? _____

I tallied my arms! I have ₩ arms! You have \|\| arms.
The total tally is ₩ \|\| arms!

DINO-MITE!

Here are names of ten dinosaurs. **Write how many letters are in each name.**

Allosaurus	☐ letters	Stegosaurus	☐ letters
Barosaurus	☐ letters	Stygimoloch	☐ letters
Corythosaurus	☐ letters	Triceratops	☐ letters
Iguanodon	☐ letters	Troodon	☐ letters
Microraptor	☐ letters	Velociraptor	☐ letters

Make a bar chart. Color in a box for each dinosaur to show the number of letters in its name.

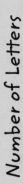

The Number of Letters in Dinosaur Names

Number of Letters										
12 or more										
11 letters										
10 letters										
9 letters										
8 letters										
7 or less										
	1	2	3	4	5	6	7	8	9	10

Number of Dinosaurs

How many letters are there in the most names? _____

How many dinosaurs have names with 8 letters? _____

Add a dinosaur name. _____

Count the letters in the name and add it to the chart.

Just a Minute

What can you do in a minute? **Make an X.**

Kate is Late!

Kate is always one hour late. Look at each clock.
Then draw the hour hand one hour later.

Shirley is one hour early! Look at the clock. **Then draw the hour hand one hour earlier.**

TIME Travel!

Look at the time! **Draw a path to the clock that is** one hour later.

11:00

1:30

2:30

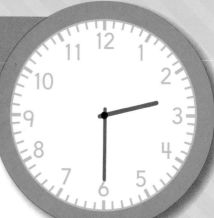

Draw a path to the clock that is a half hour later.

4:00

6:30

8:30

Is it half past the hour? Then the minute hand points to the 6. Is it half past 8? Then it's my bedtime! Goodnight!

Time Pattern

Look for the pattern. **Circle the clock that comes next!**

Geometry

BUILDaB[ROBOT]T!

You can build your own robot! Follow the directions to collect the shapes you need.

Color in shapes that are not curved.

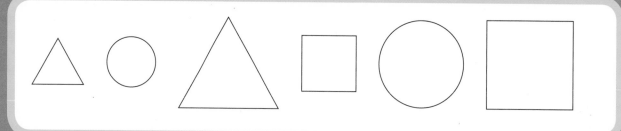

Color in shapes with 4 corners.

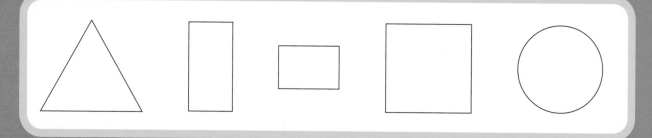

Color in shapes with more than 3 sides.

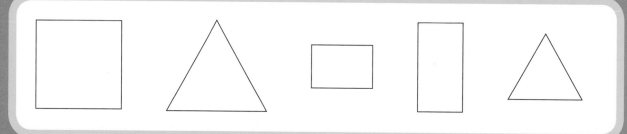

Color in curved shapes.

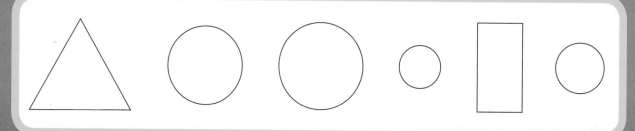

My Robot

What will your robot's name be? _____

Draw your robot using each shape you colored in.
There should be **14 shapes** total.

Get In 3-D Shape!

Three dimensional, or 3-D, shapes have height, width, and depth. Some 3-D shapes have a flat surface.

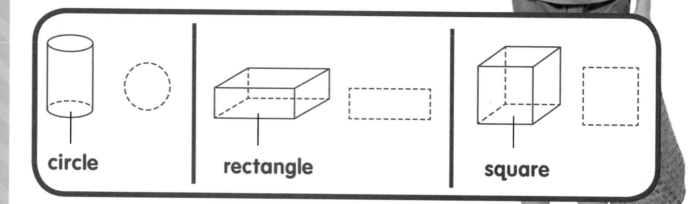

circle

rectangle

square

Kyle traced these shapes. **Draw a line to the object he used to trace each shape.**

What shape can you make if you trace these? Draw it!

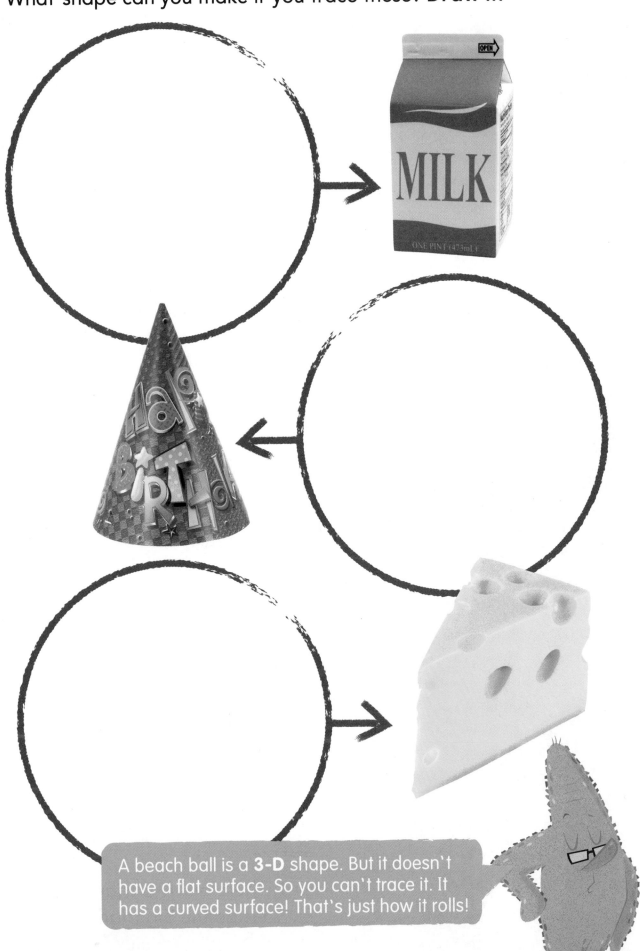

A beach ball is a **3-D** shape. But it doesn't have a flat surface. So you can't trace it. It has a curved surface! That's just how it rolls!

BIG SHAPE! ⟫⟫⟫⟫⟫⟫⟫⟫⟫

A big shape can be made of many little shapes!
This big rectangle is made of 70 little squares!

How many triangles do you see inside the big triangle?

Hint: There are two triangle sizes inside the big triangle.

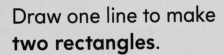

Little Shape!

Draw one line to make
two rectangles.

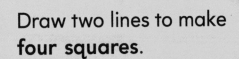

Draw two lines to make
four squares.

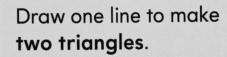

Draw one line to make
two triangles.

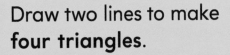

Draw two lines to make
four triangles.

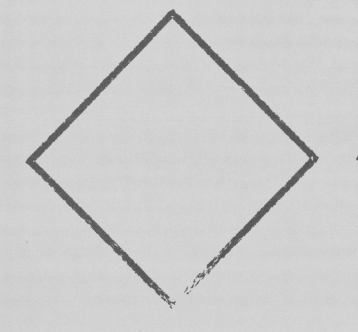

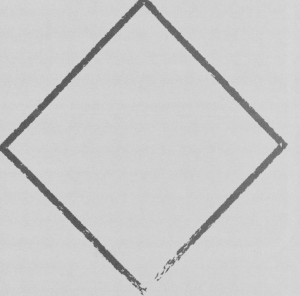

BLOCK ARCHITECT!

Gary wants to be an architect. He stacks blocks to make small buildings. **Which building can he make with the blocks shown?**

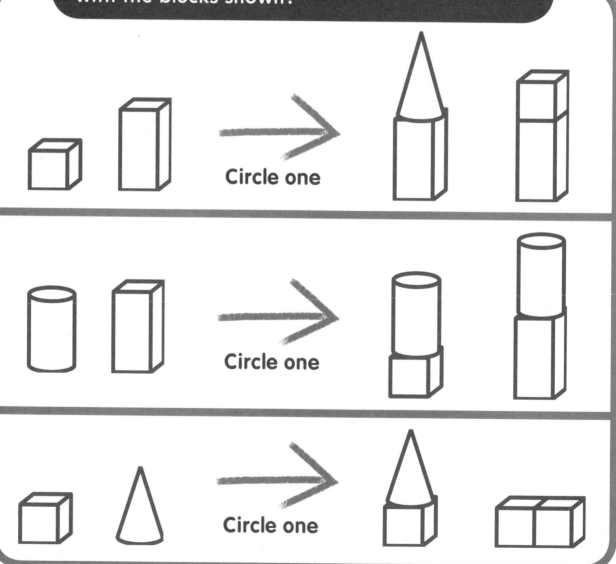

Circle one

Circle one

Circle one

Shape SHIFTER

You can combine shapes to make a new shape!

2 shapes   **combine**   **new shape**

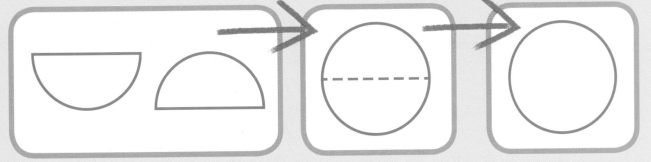

Circle two shapes you can combine to make the new shape!

Take

Zach wants to build a fast paper airplane!
To do it, he must fold the paper into equal parts.
Circle the shapes that show equal parts.

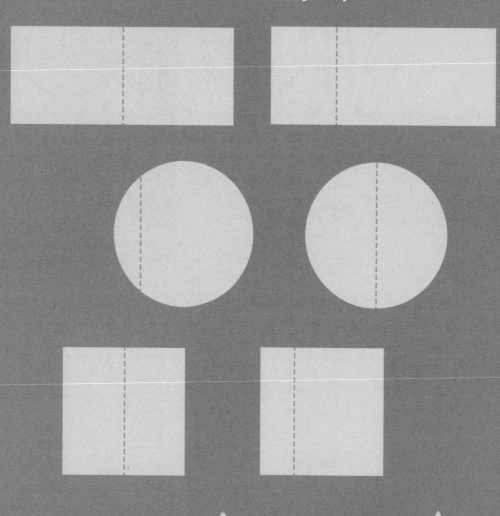

Flight!

Zach already folded these.
Draw the other half to show
what they look like unfolded.

Better Half

Twin sisters Violet and Vivian always split their treats! **Circle the treats that are equal halves.**

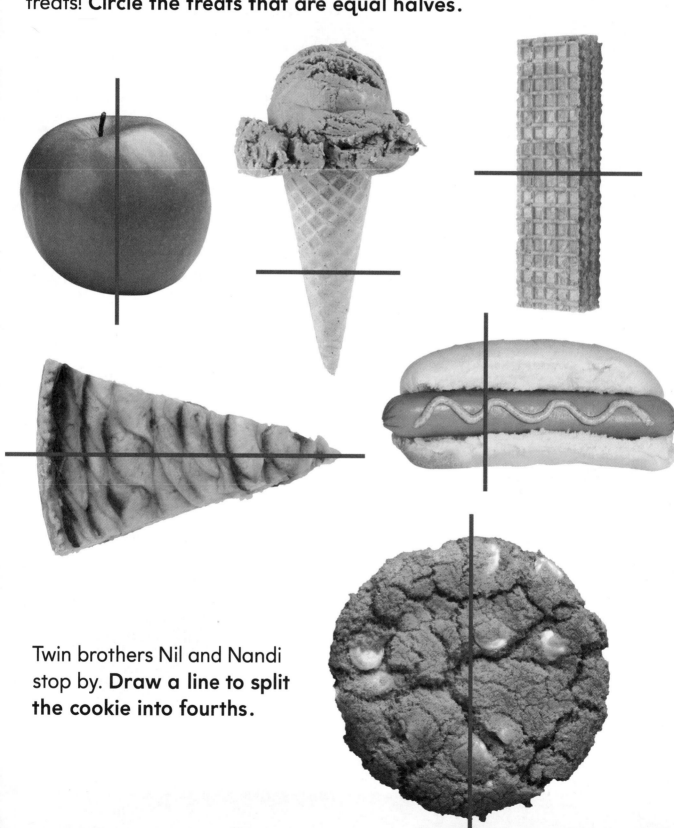

Twin brothers Nil and Nandi stop by. **Draw a line to split the cookie into fourths.**

Doghouse Depot!

Grandma Dean is building a doghouse. **Circle the wood that is cut into thirds.** Thirds are three equal parts.

Grandma Dean wants to cut this wood into thirds. **Draw cut lines.**

227

Top It Off!

Mr. Glen's class is having a pizza party!
Cut the pizzas **into equal parts.**

1 Two kids share this pizza.
Draw a line to cut it into halves.

2 Four kids share this pizza.
Draw lines to cut it into fourths.

3 Eight kids share this pizza.
Draw lines to cut it into eighths.

Hope and Lex share a pizza. Only Lex wants pepperoni.

Draw **pepperoni on half the pizza.**

Circle **the side that Lex will eat.**

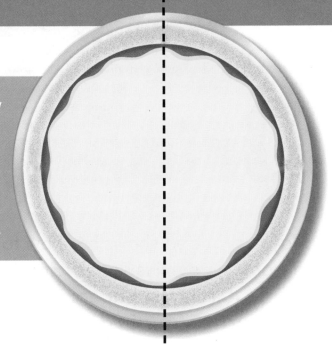

Marla and Jeremy share a pepperoni pizza. Only Jeremy wants mushrooms.

Draw **pepperoni on the whole pizza. Draw mushrooms on half the pizza.**

Circle **the side that Marla will eat.**

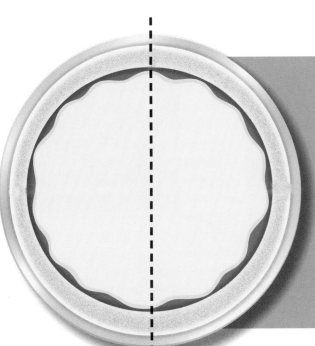

Dale and Lev share a pizza. Only Dale wants pepperoni. Only Lev wants olives.

Draw **the toppings on the pizza.**

Circle **the side that Lev will eat.**

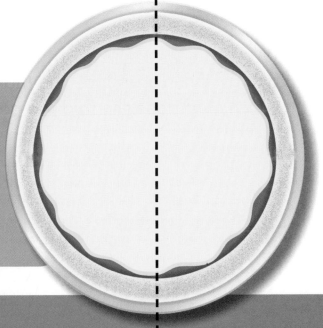

Oh, Origami!

Maya's grandpa shows her how to make origami. Origami is paper folded into fun shapes. **Circle the papers that are folded into fourths.** Fourths are four equal parts.

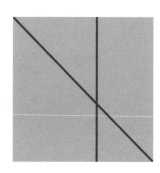

Maya loves her grandpa. She makes him an origami heart. In which step does she fold the paper into fourths? **Circle it.**

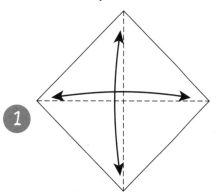
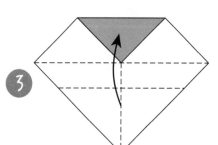

Nature of Science

FIVE SENSATIONAL SENSES

2

Does cheese smell **stinky**?
Does a worm feel **slimy**?

You use your senses every day to learn about the world!

Name the sense being used in each picture.

3

1 smell

4

5

The five senses are **sight, hearing, smell, taste,** and **touch.**

232

What is the last thing you sensed?

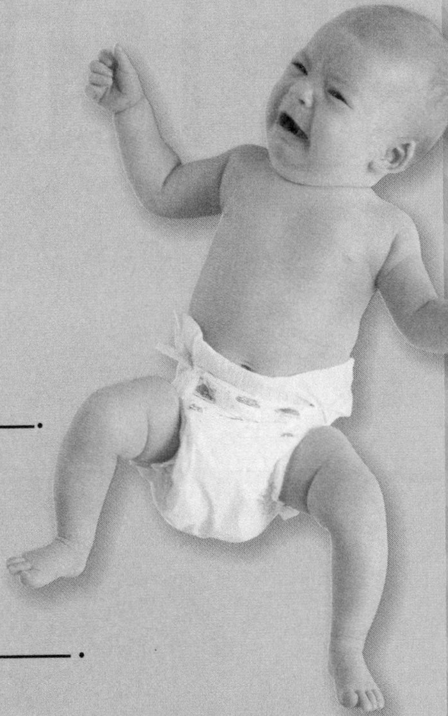

I heard a ___baby cry___. It was ___loud___.

I smelled a _____. It was _____.

I tasted a _____. It was _____.

I touched a _____. It was _____.

Which is your favorite sense? Why?

My favorite sense is _____.

I love to _____!

THE RiGht TOOL

Which tool would you use to find the answer?
Draw a line from the picture to the tool.

Who weighs more?
Francine or Teddy?

Is the water warm
enough for Bubbles?

How many legs does
this tiny critter have?

Did my sister get a bigger
slice of pizza than I did?

FOR THE Job

Which tools are **not** used to **measure**?
Cross them out!

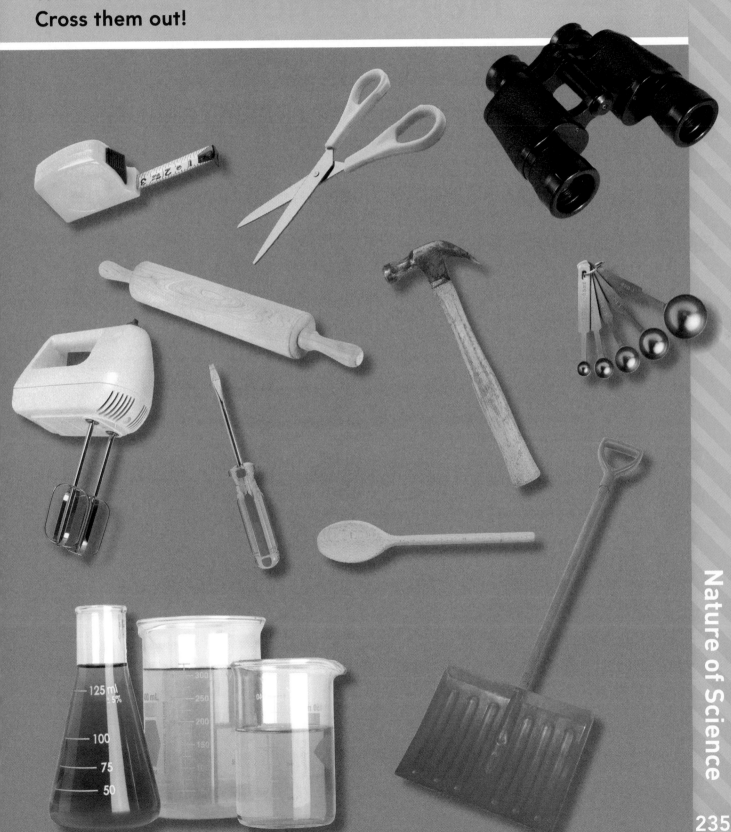

My Mighty
Measurements

Find a ruler or tape measure.
Measure your arm, hand, foot, and nose.
Measure again using a paperclip!

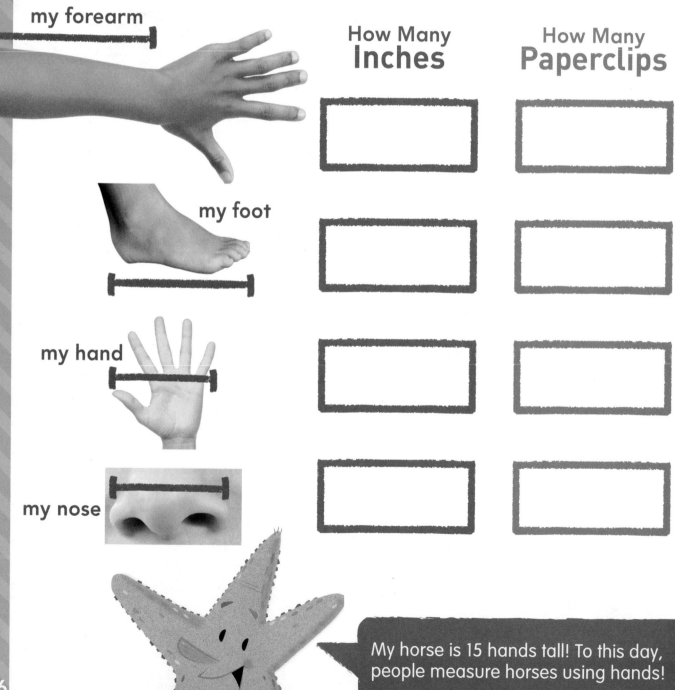

my forearm

my foot

my hand

my nose

How Many Inches	How Many Paperclips

My horse is 15 hands tall! To this day, people measure horses using hands!

236

Life
Science

CREATURE FEATURE

Unscramble the letters to name six animal groups.
Then draw a line to the animal in that group.

ihsf _fish_

rdib _____

mlamam _____

senict _____

elerpti _____

pahmianbi _____

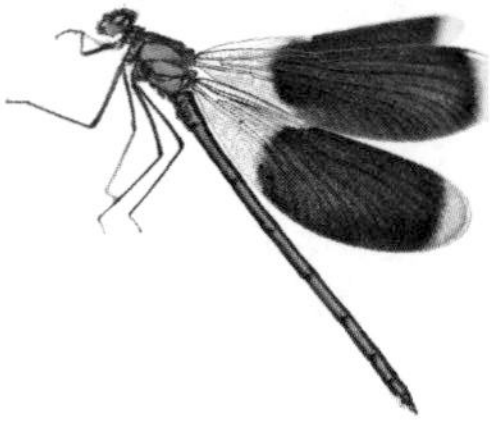

238

Animals on the Move

Does a bug do the backstroke? One way to group animals is by how they move. Make an X in a box to show how each animal moves.

How Does It Move?

	Walk	Swim	Fly
duck			
butterfly			
mouse			
fish			
bat			
penguin			
parrot			
alligator			
cow			

Which animal above moves in all **three** ways? _____

What's another way an animal can move? _____

(Hint: Monkeys and geckos do this to go up!)

Some people call me a starfish, but I'm not a fish. Fish move with their tails. I use tiny, tubed feet to get around.

Give Me SHELTER!

Animals need a safe place to live.
Match the animals below to a shelter.

A _____ lives in a den.

A _____ lives in a burrow.

A _____ lives in a lodge.

A _____ lives in a tube tent.

A _____ lives in an anemone.

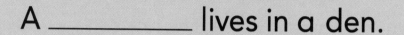

beaver   clownfish   prairie dog   skunk   tarantula

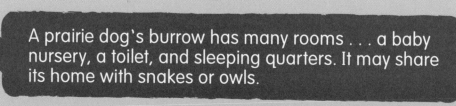

A prairie dog's burrow has many rooms . . . a baby nursery, a toilet, and sleeping quarters. It may share its home with snakes or owls.

LIVING IT UP!

Living things **grow** and **change**. They also need food, air, and water. **Circle each living thing. Draw an X on nonliving things.**

You grow and change every day.

You as a baby

You right now

Living things **reproduce**. They make new living things like themselves. But only some living things can grow back a lost arm! *Ahem*. Like me!

Junior ZOO KEEPER!

A tiger cub was born at the zoo! Can you help take care of it? You must feed it. You have to give it water. And you need to keep its home clean.

But how will you know if it feels sick? A cub can't talk!

Make an X next to each clue that a cub may be sick.

It moves less. ☐

It yawns. ☐

It eats less. ☐

It drinks more. ☐

A cub is a wild animal. But a pet cat can show the same symptoms when it is sick.

Bird
IS THE WORD

Congratulations! You discovered a new bird! The *Important Bird Society* wants to know about your bird. Circle the words that helped you **classify** it as a bird. Did it have...?

scales

fins

fur

shell

wings

hair

beak

feathers

My bird's name is

_____.

Draw your bird.

You can name your bird after yourself or someone you like! A bird scientist named Lewis's Woodpecker for Meriwether Lewis!

Junior
F REST RANGER!

A forest ranger keeps plants and animals safe. Do you want this job?

Apply here!

Draw one forest animal that you will protect.

Draw one forest plant that you will protect.

Now create a sign. Ask people not to feed animals!

Back in 1905, you only had to be able to ride a horse and read a map to be a forest ranger. Today, most rangers know how to fight fires!

FIDO
Has Needs, Too

Think of a pet. Write the pet's name below and what kind of animal it is. Make a list of what it needs to live. Then, explain how those needs get met.

Name:	
Type:	
Needs	How needs get met
water	
food	

Wild animals need food, water, and safe places to live. Why is a nest a safe home for a bird?

WHO ? EATS WHOM ?

A food chain shows who eats whom (or what)! First, the carrot used sunlight to make food. Then, you ate the carrot!

What is the order of this food chain?
Write 1, 2, and 3. Number 3 is the guy who eats last!

UUURP! Excuse me! I just ate a clam. Before that, the clam ate plankton. Before that, the plankton used sun to make food. What's for dessert?

Happy Plants!

A plant grows when it gets what it needs. **Circle the right word to take care of your plant!**

I give it   water   seeds

I put it near a window so it can get

sunlight   air

My plant is growing! I will move it to a bigger container so it can get enough nutrients from the

pot   soil

Uh-oh! This plant is not getting what it needs. Circle what it needs.

Even underwater plants need sunshine. That's why algae can be deadly! It blocks sunshine. Plants below the surface can't make food!

MADE TO ORDER

Everything we wear, watch, and toss is made of materials.

Circle items that are made with **natural** materials. (A natural material is found in nature!)

socks

cotton swab

fork

lunchbox

book

248

clay pot

wooden toy

sunglasses

ruler

You can recycle items made with natural and human-made materials.
Circle items made from **human-made** materials.

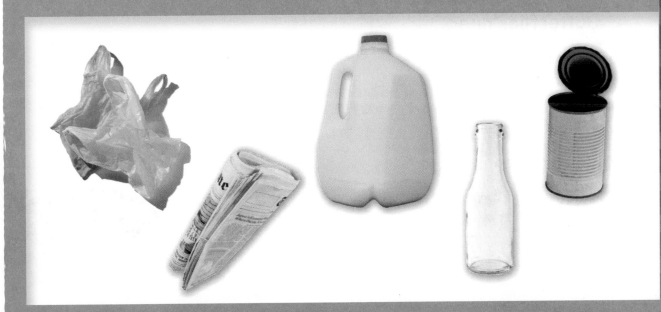

Butterfly Garden!

The city asks you to design a butterfly garden.

Draw a design for the garden.

_____'s Butterfly Garden

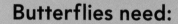

Butterflies need:

- Sunny places to be warm
- Shade to keep cool
- Colorful flowers for food
- Rocks to rest on
- Puddles or birdbaths for water

Earth
Science

EARTH TO Elda!

Space girl Stella is visiting Earth. Read the postcard she wrote to her sister.

Dear Elda,

I am writing to you from Earth! There are many different places to live!

I visited a rain forest. It is a wet environment. Birds and monkeys live in the tall trees. I saw a monkey eat a bug!

I also visited a desert! It is a dry environment. I saw a Gila monster! It lives below the rocky ground. It ate a small bird!

xo, Stella

Why is the rain forest a good environment for a monkey? Circle words that Stella uses to describe its **shelter** and **food.**

Why is the desert a good environment for a Gila monster? Underline words that Stella uses to describe its **shelter** and **food.**

What is your environment like?
Describe where you live to a friend in space.

Dear _____

_____

_____

_____

_____

xo,

_____

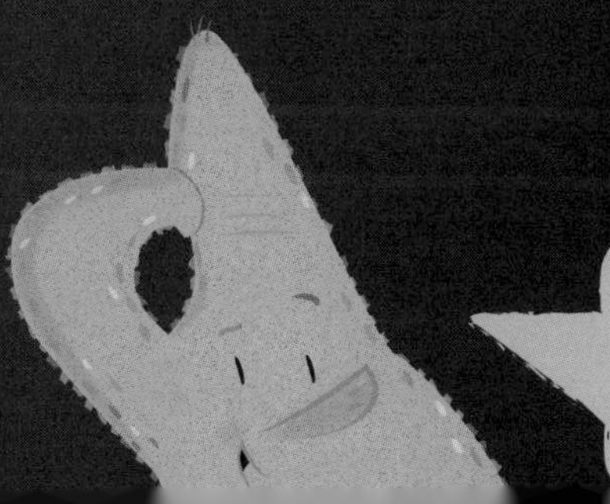

The ocean is my oyster! I enjoy living on the ocean floor.
That's where my food is! Oysters and clams. *Mmm!*

WHERE IS Stella?

Space girl Elda can see Earth from space!
Help her understand what she sees.
Circle the parts that are land.
Draw waves on the parts that are water.

Elda's sister is visiting a **tundra** this week.
A tundra is very cold. There is a lot of snow.
Where do you think the tundra is? **Draw an arrow.**

Did you draw a lot of waves? Most of Earth is covered with water. That's good. There are 2,000 types of sea stars. And we need to stretch out!

NATURE'S GOODIES

Say each natural resource.
Write how it is being used.

We use **air**

to ___breathe___ .

We use **plants**

for _____ .

We use **water**

to _____ .

We use **soil**

to _____ .

We use **animals**

for _____ .

We use **rocks**

to _____ .

This book is made of a natural resource. Which one?

WHERE'S THE water?

The piranha lives in fresh water. **Draw a path to the fresh water river.**

The shark lives in salty water. **Draw a path to the ocean.**

piranha

shark

river

ocean

Fresh water fish live in lakes, rivers, and streams in North America. Scientists worry that two of five fresh water fish may not survive. **Draw an X over two fish.**

Some fish live in both fresh water and salty water!
They are called anadromous fish.

AN-A-DROM-OUS

A salmon is anadromous!
It lives in a fresh water stream as a baby.
It moves to the ocean when it grows up!

Circle the salmon that are ready to move to the ocean.

I've never met a goldfish. They only live in fresh water.

BE A WATER HER○!

People, animals, and plants need water to stay healthy. How does your family use water? **Circle the ways.**

HOW WILL **YOU** PROTECT WATER?

☐ **I WILL** turn off a dripping faucet.

☐ **I WILL NEVER** litter.

☐ **I WILL** use less water for baths and showers.

Safety!

Have you ever been to a pool, a beach, or lake?

Draw a 〰️ under the ways you stay safe in or near water.

I learned to swim.

I wear a life jacket.

I swim with someone else.

I leave the water if I hear thunder.

I never dive in shallow water.

What can the people do to be safe?
Draw on the picture.

Too many people are in a boat. The lifeguard says, "It's not safe! Three must get out!" Three people leave the boat. Now five are in the boat. How many were there to start?

Pollution stinks!

Pollution is waste that harms air, water, and land. What type of pollution do you see?
Is it air, water, or land?

water

_____

_____

_____

Whales, dolphins, and turtles eat plastic garbage. They think it is food! It can make them very sick.

GOOD AS NEW!

Rex, Rory, and Rayna love Earth. They always reduce, reuse, and recycle. **Write the best words in each blank.**

Rex turns off the water while he brushes.

He _____!

Rory brings his lunch in the same bag.

He _____!

Rayna puts cans into the right bin.

She _____!

How do you reduce, reuse, and recycle?

I use less _____.

I use my _____ again and again.

I recycled a _____.
Now it can be turned into something new!

Are there items in your home that can be reused or recycled? Look for them with your mom or dad!

THE SCOOP ON SOIL

Soil is made of bits of rock, dead plants, and animals. Soils can be different colors.

Circle the scoop of black soil.

Iron is a reddish metal.
Cross out the scoop that has iron.

Soil Puzzle! Soil can get tired! Some farmers used to plant the same crop every year. Plants stopped growing. George Washington Carver was a teacher and scientist. He taught farmers to rotate crops.

Year 1: Plant cotton

Year 2: Plant sweet potatoes

Year 3: Plant cotton

What should a farmer plant in year 7?

CLEAN UP, CLEAN UP, EVERYBODY!

Earth does not sneeze. But it can show signs that it's sick!
Help Earth feel better!

| air | bikes | cans | land | trash | water |

People ride _____.

This keeps the _____ clean.

People keep _____ out of the river.

This keeps the _____ clean.

People throw trash in _____.

This keeps the _____ clean.

What's the Weather, Heather?

Sometimes Heather feels sweaty. Other times, her eyelashes freeze! **Help Heather learn how to dress.**

rain

sun

snow

Draw clothing and shoes to match the weather.

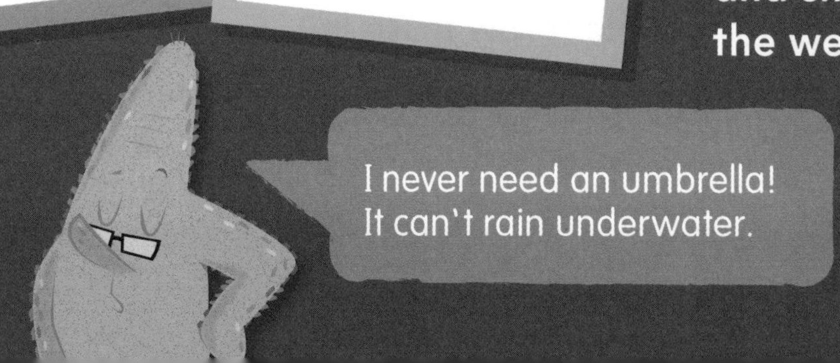

I never need an umbrella! It can't rain underwater.

NAKED TREES,
TREES WITH CLOTHES

A **season** is a time of year.

The weather changes with each season.

That can change the way trees look.

Look at the trees.
Write what season it is.

Some trees look the same all year long.
Guess what they're called. *Evergreens*!

White, Wet, or Windy?

Draw a picture showing the weather. Then **guess** what the weather will be tomorrow!

Were you right?

		observe **today is**	predict **tomorrow is**
clear			
cloudy			
rainy			
cold			
windy			

Can fish predict weather? There is a saying: "Trout jump high when a rain is nigh!" What do you think this means?

Physical Science

WISH UPON A Star

Look up at the sky!

Draw what you see during the day. Then draw the sky at night.

day	night

Unscramble the letters to make each sentence.

tasr   A _____ gives off its own light.

omon   The _____ is a large ball of rock.

It is not a star!

usn   The _____ is a star we can see

in the day.

Sometimes, you can't see the sun. Where did it go? *Nowhere!* The sun doesn't move. It's hiding behind the clouds!

CLEAN UP YOUR MATTER!

Did you leave your matter lying around?
A **solid** keeps its shape.
A **liquid** takes the shape of its container.
A **gas** fills all the space in its container.

Which type of matter is each thing below?

I'm a solid who lives in a liquid. *Poot!*
Excuse me. Sometimes, I also get gas.

▶PUSH It ◀PULL It

A force makes something move or stop moving.
Push and **pull** are forces.

How do you move the things below?
Do you **push** or **pull** them?

 I _____ the shopping cart.

 I _____ off the ground.

 I _____ the rope.

 I _____ the doorbell.

Gravity is a force that pulls us down.
Gravity is what pulls you down the slide.
Wheee!

Listen UP!

Sounds can give us information.
Circle the sounds that warn us of danger!

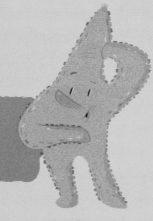

Sound is made when an object **vibrates**. When you bang a drum, it vibrates! When you talk, you vibrate! Touch your throat and hum! Can you feel it buzz?

find the SOLUTION

Sammy Salt mixes with the matter below.
In each, does he **dissolve**?
Or does he become part of a **mixture**?
Circle the answer.

  **dissolve**   **mixture**

  **dissolve**   **mixture**

  **dissolve**   **mixture**

Salt can mix with a solid or a liquid. When salt mixes with a liquid, it **dissolves**. It becomes something new! The new thing is called a **solution**. Salt water is a solution.

Community

This Land Is

Where do you live? **Circle the state you live in.** Then draw a star on each state you have visited.

My state is _____.

About the same number of people live in Massachusetts and Arizona. Which state is more crowded?

Your Land

What kind of land is shown in this state? **Circle one.**

beach   mountains   prairie   desert   canyons   swamps

What kinds of land are in your state? _____

A Mouse On

A mouse visits your house. Give the mouse directions.
Write north, east, south, or west.

Are you hungry? Go _____ of the couch.

Beware! Do not go _____ of the couch.

What time is it? Look _____ of the couch.

It's time to watch *Downton Mice.* The TV is _____ of the couch.

the Couch

The mouse wants water. Draw a glass of water north of the couch.

The mouse needs a pillow. Draw a pillow east of the mouse.

The Key to Fruitville

Some keys open locks. Others help us use maps. Look at the symbols in the map. The key tells you what each symbol means.

Map Key  House School

 Library  Park

Rhubarb Road

Strawberry Street

Circle the school symbol in the key. Draw a line from the symbol to the school on the map.

What street is the park on? _____

What street is the library on? _____

Mr. Mulberry is moving to Fruitville with Mara, his daughter. He wants Mara to walk to school without crossing any streets. Circle the houses he may like.

Mr. Mulberry is a veterinarian. He opens an animal hospital on Rhubarb Road. Add a symbol to the key for an animal hospital. Then add it to the map.

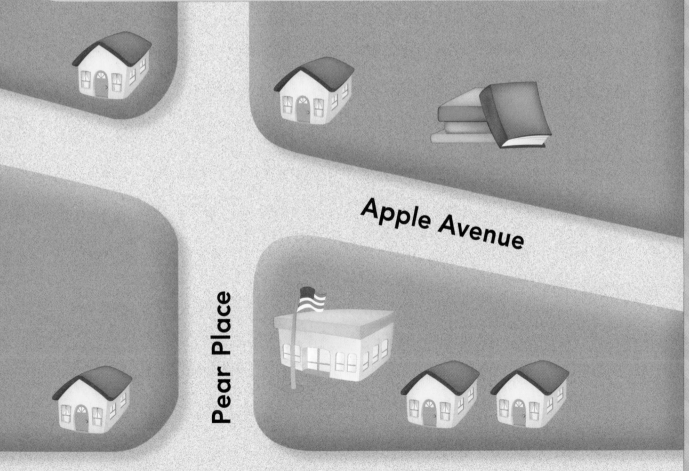

Apple Avenue

Pear Place

A FLAG for

Find your state's flag on the Internet! Draw it below.

Why does your flag have the colors or symbols it does?

YOU!

What would your family's flag look like? Think about your family's favorite stories, sports, or foods!

Draw your family's flag.

I ♥ Symbols

A **symbol** stands for something else. A symbol can be an object, a building, or a song. Some symbols stand for the United States. **Circle them.**

The maple leaf is a symbol of Canada.

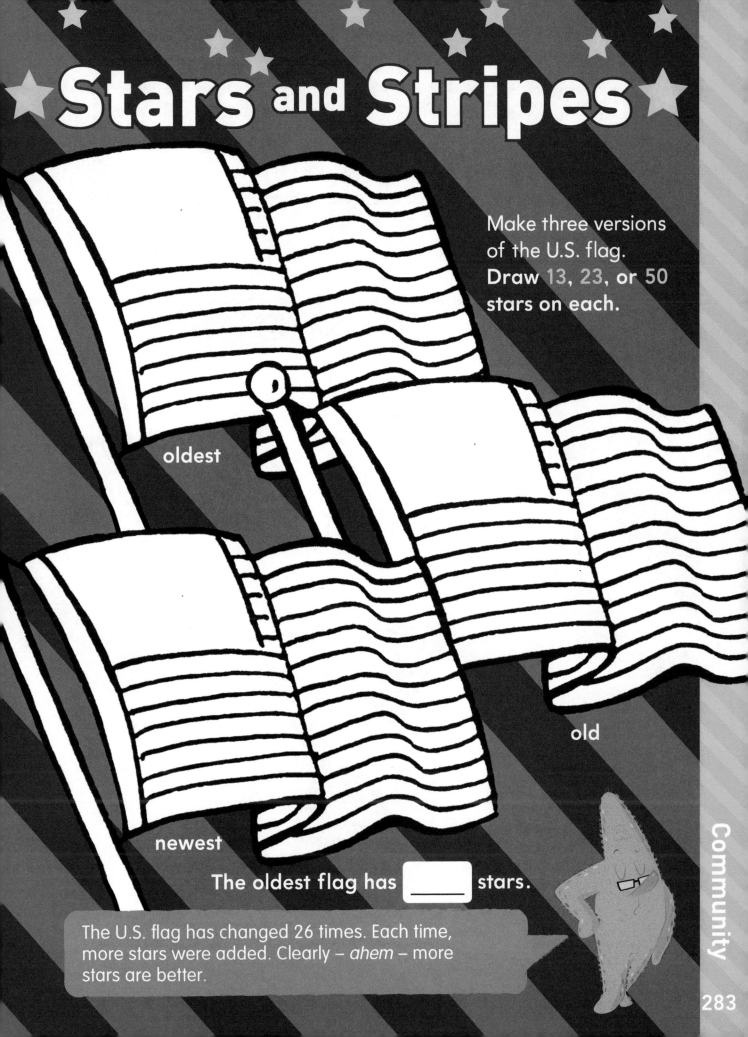

★ Stars and Stripes ★

Make three versions of the U.S. flag. Draw 13, 23, or 50 stars on each.

oldest

old

newest

The oldest flag has _____ **stars.**

The U.S. flag has changed 26 times. Each time, more stars were added. Clearly – *ahem* – more stars are better.

Happy National
HOLIDAY!

A national holiday is special. It is a day the nation celebrates together. **Write the name of the holiday on each postcard.**

Happy _____ Day!

Happy _____ Day!

Join the CELEBRATION!

Kids in other countries celebrate holidays. Maybe one day you will celebrate a holiday in another country!

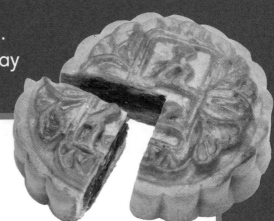

Shen eats a mooncake on Chinese Thanksgiving.

What do you eat on Thanksgiving?

_____

Lin waves a dragon at the parade.

What do you wave at a parade?

_____

Jia decorates her home during the Chinese New Year.

How do you decorate your home on a holiday?

_____

_____

Write a postcard to Yuan in China. Tell Yuan about your favorite holiday. Do you dress up? Do you eat special food? Do you listen to special music?

Dear Yuan

Dear Yuan,

My favorite holiday is _____.

_____

_____

_____

Your friend,

_____

May Days

Which month does the calendar show? _____

On which day of the week is May Day? _____

If today is May 6, what day is tomorrow? _____

If today is May 20, what day was yesterday? _____

May						
Sunday	Monday	Tuesday	Wednesday	Thursday	Friday	Saturday
				1 May Day	2	3
4	5 Cinco de Mayo	6	7	8	9	10
11 Mother's Day	12	13	14	15	16	17
18	19	20	21	22	23	24
25	26 Memorial Day	27	28	29	30	31

WITH Liberty AND Justice FOR ALL

hero

landmarks

flag

freedom

Our _____ has stars and stripes. It reminds us of the _____ we have in our country. Sometimes we fly the flag when we want to honor a _____ for doing something brave and important. Some heroes are honored with _____ that we can visit.

This landmark honors President _____.

A Hero Is...

A hero tries to make life better for someone else.

invents   protects   stands up

A hero _ _ _ _ _ _ _ _ for equal rights.

A hero _ _ _ _ _ _ _ _ people, animals, and Earth.

A hero _ _ _ _ _ _ _ things to make life safer or easier.

Sometimes we name streets after heroes. Who is your hero?
Write the name on the street sign.

DR KING DR

A hero is not always famous. My cousin Gareth is a
hero. He rescued a dogfish that ran away from home.

Follow the RULES

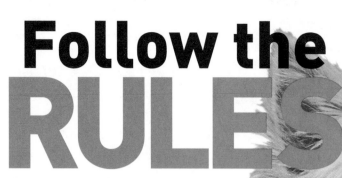

Rules can keep us safe.
Some rules are...

Buckle up!

Wash your hands.

Keep your dog on a leash.

What does Samuel need to stay safe outside? **Circle it.**

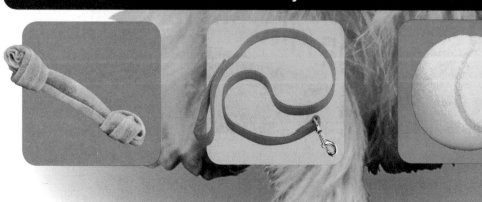

It's a Sign!

Signs are everywhere! They give us information. They tell us how to be safe. **Circle the sign that tells you a train is coming.**

How can a sign keep you safe?

_____

_____

Maybe someone put you in charge of your little brother or sister. But other people are in charge of *you*! Who are they?

Who Is in Charge?

| mayor | lifeguard | coach | teacher |

A _____ tells the team how to play.

A _____ tells swimmers how to be safe.

A _____ is in charge of a town or city.

A _____ tells students what to do.

Your mom tells you to _____.
She is in charge.

292

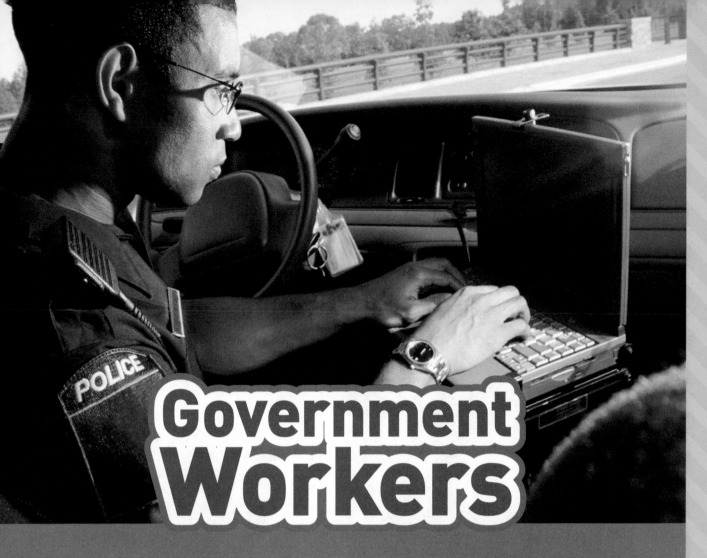

Government Workers

These people work for the government.

firefighter   police officer   president   ranger   teacher

The _____ keeps plants and animals safe.

The _____ makes sure people follow laws.

The _____ stops fires.

The _____ helps students learn.

The _____ is the country's leader.

A Good Citizen

A citizen is a person who belongs to a community. You are a citizen.

Citizens have rights and responsibilities. A **right** is a freedom. A **responsibility** is something you *should* do. Make an X next to responsibilities.

☐ Do homework

☐ Own a pet

☐ Recycle

☐ Ride a bike

The government protects your civil rights. One civil right is the freedom to say whatever is on your mind. Like, *Nachos!*

Right to Vote

Voting is an important right. It helps people make big decisions, like who will run the country! It can also help make small decisions, like what pet you should get!

Ask each family member to vote. Write their names. Make an X next to the pet they want.

A New Family Pet				
	Pot-Bellied Pig	Python	Piranha	Pygmy Goat
You				

Add up the votes.

The winner is _____

THEN and NOW

Look at each picture. Draw a new picture to show how we do it today.

Call for help!

There is a fire! Run to the fire alarm box. Pull the handle.

Talk to a friend.

Dan talks on the phone.

Write a letter.

Kay writes to Wilma.

Take a picture.

Cheryl takes a picture.

My Timeline

You started off a baby. And now you're a kid! What happened in between?

Circle your age now.

| 0 | 1 | 2 | 3 | 4 |

I was born.

_____

_____

_____

_____

_____

Draw important things that happened to you. How old were you? Draw a line from the picture to the age. Then describe each picture.

| 5 | 6 | 7 | 8 | 9 |

_____

_____

    _____

    _____

        _____

        _____

Here are ideas: When did you learn to walk? Lose your first tooth? Start school? Win a trophy?

Teri's Timeline

Monday	Tuesday	Wednesday	Thursday	Friday

President's Day (No school!)	Soccer	My birthday!	Dentist	Field trip

Teri's timeline shows _____ days.

Teri did not go to school on _____. It was _____.

She played soccer on _____.

Teri brought a cake to school on _____.

On Thursday, she went to _____.

The last thing on the timeline happens on _____.

Hello, Future

technology   past   change   communicate   present

Places, schools, and transportation _____ over time.

In the _____, kids dipped pens into ink to write. In the

_____, we use pens. _____ helps people travel

faster and more safely. It also changes how we _____,

or the way we share ideas and feelings.

Make a Sandwich

Label the flowchart to show
how to make a peanut butter
and jelly sandwich.

_____
- -
_____

_____
- -
_____

_____
- -
_____

_____
- -
_____

Marketplace

Serving the Needs of Many

Some workers sell **services**. Services are kinds of work people do for money. **Draw a line from each service to a person.**

dentist

mechanic

- I can fix your car.
- I can clean your teeth.
- I can drive you to school.
- I can take your dog for a walk.
- I can cut your hair.

dog walker

barber

bus driver

Good Cereal!

Goods are things people make or grow to sell.

Count the goods on the table.

There are _____ goods.

Make a new cereal. **Draw it!**

GOODS and SERVICES

Bruno uses money to buy goods and services for his dog. He made a list. **Make an X next to goods on the list.**

☐ Take dog to vet

☐ Get dog food

☐ Get dog toy

☐ Get new collar

☐ Take dog to groomer

☒ _____

Add one more good to the list. What will Bruno buy?

Baker's Basket

Dale sells baked goods. The graph shows how many muffin baskets he sold.

Baskets of Muffins Sold	
Blueberry	🧁🧁🧁🧁🧁🧁🧁
Oat bran	🧁🧁🧁
Banana	🧁

 = one basket

Dale sold more _____ muffins than any other

flavor. Dale sold three baskets of _____

muffins. _____ is the least popular flavor.

Altogether, Dale sold _____ baskets.

If one basket holds 10 muffins, how many muffins did Dale sell altogether?

Birthday Budget

card ($2)

purse ($15)

balloon ($3)

card ($5)

Lisa wants to buy a present for her mom.

She has $20. She wants to buy a gift, a card, and wrapping paper. **Circle the things she should buy.**

earrings ($25)

mug ($10)

wrapping paper ($2)

plant ($18)

How much did you spend? _____ dollars

Why did you choose these things?

_____

MONEY MOVES

Complete the chart to show how money moves.

_____ sells lemonade.

_____ buys lemonade from _____.

_____ buys a plant from _____.

_____ pays
_____ to fix his car.

Clues

Albert has a garden.

Amy has a lemonade stand.   Tina is a mechanic.

Volunteers

A volunteer works without pay to help people, animals, or the environment. Some kids collect food for animals in shelters. Others make holiday cards for senior citizens.

Color in the heart next to things you care about.

♡ I want to help animals.

♡ I want to stop bullying.

♡ I want to help people read.

♡ I want to help the environment.

♡ I want to help senior citizens.

Ask your mom and dad how you can help!

Answer Key

PHONICS

p. 8

b under bee, bear, butterfly
d under dog, dragonfly
f under flamingo, frog

p. 9

Correct path is through heart, jar, and kite

p. 10

l under lion, lawnmover
m under maracas, monkey, mask
p under pickles, popcorn, pogo stick

p. 11

Correct path is through quarter, queen, and quilt

p. 12

r under roller skate, rowboat
s under scooter, sailboat
t under train, truck

p. 13

v matched to vase
w matched to walrus
x matched to xylophone
y matched to yo-yo
z matched to zebra

p. 14

Circle apple, cat, anteater, bat, can

p. 15

Circle acorn, rake, lake, apron, milk shake

p. 16

Correct path is through bell, eggplant, and exclamation point

p. 17

Correct stones are bee, tree, and deer

p. 18

Words are pig, wig, snake, sad, red, six, kitten, mitt, dig
Circled words are pig, wig, mitt, six, kitten, dig

p. 19

Words are kite, lips, ice / drum, dice, bike / mug, mice, cake
Circled words are kite, ice, dice, bike, mice

p. 20

flop, pop matched with top
dot, cot matched with pot
rock, sock matched with lock
hog, frog, matched with dog

p. 21

flow, row matched with bow and arrow
oh, no matched with yo-yo
oat, goat matched with boat
rose, toes matched with nose

p. 22

juice, ruler, cup, music, sun, bug, emu, cube

p. 23

Circled/written words are butterfly, truck, cup, duck, bug, skunk

pp. 24–25

Words are cherry, ship, cheese, shade, throne, three, chocolate, shapes

p. 26

Under sponge circle sp and the written word should be springy
Under snail circle sn and the written word should be slimy
Under snake circle sn and the written word should be scaly
Under spider circle sp and the written word should be scary
Under sloth circle sl and the written word should be slow
Under skunk circle the sk and the written word should be smelly

p. 27

Under frog circle fr
Under grapes circle gr
Under truck circle tr
Under pretzel circle pr
Under crown circle cr
Under fruit circle fr

p. 28

Under cloud circle cl
Under sled circle sl
Under slide circle sl
Under flowers circle fl
Under plane circle pl

p. 29

kid	rib
crab	sled
weed	web
crib	bird

p. 30

Connect the mouse and the monkey

p. 31

mom	pen
tan	swim
fan	drum
can	clam
pin	man

pp. 32–33

Words are map, bug, stick, log, tent, sun, hot dog

p. 34

brain on a plate
nails on a lake
snail on a cake

p. 35

soft c: circle, city
hard c: car, crab
soft g: germ, giant
hard g: grass, gold

p. 36

dime	lime
sign	fly
pie	mind

p. 37

toad	nose
road	coat
rose	home
toes	

p. 38

long i sounds are spy, sky, fly
long e sounds are fairy, berry, pony

p. 39

words drawn to ue guy: blue, cute, tune
words drawn to oo guy: moon, tooth, boots, spoon

p. 40

plane	train
brick	glue
slide	grapes
skates	star

SPELLING AND VOCABULARY

p. 42

is, are, see, We, us, like

p. 43

my, me, I, him, does, all, He

p. 45

He, his, They, her, She, Their, it, Answer will vary.

pp. 46–47

Answers will vary.

p. 48

under 1, one, 2, two, 3, three, 4, four, 5, five, 6, six, 7, seven, 8, eight, 9, nine

p. 49

each word colored the right colors, red, blue, orange, purple, yellow, white, green, black, pink, brown.

pp. 50–51

kick, sing, ride, run
dance, paint, drum

p. 52

Down: 1. sink 2. chair 3. table
Across: 4. lamp 5. kitchen 6. rug

p. 53

Draw lines from words to photos:
flag to flag
teacher to teacher
student to student
book to book
backpack to backpack
pencil to pencil

p. 54

p. 55

sad	mad
scared	sleepy
sick	happy
silly	

p. 56

snail	robot
shell	plum
kite	flag
unicorn	boot
lamp	octopus
rug	lion
fish	family

GRAMMAR AND MECHANICS

pp. 58–59

dad, boy, dog, kite, balloon, mailbox, ice cream, girl, cat

pp. 60–61

wheel, aquarium, windowsill, bird cage
hamster, turtle, cat, canary

pp. 62–63

apples, bananas, carrots, oranges, pears, broccoli, grapes, celery
Fruit and vegetables should match labeled carts.

pp. 64–65

mountains
farm
beach
desert
home

p. 66

Kim, Mom / Kim, Green Day School / Joan / Kim, Laura / Carson Zoo / Kim, Laura / Stan Bock / Bird House / Talking Birds / Kim, Kim / Kim

p. 67

Carly, North Dakota,
Lieutenant Davis, Amazon,
Mount Kilimanjaro, Statue of Liberty

p. 68

juggles, flies, lifts, walks, jumps, cheers

p. 69

jump, drive, ride

pp. 70–71

small, clean, dark, happy, dry

pp. 72–73

red, prickly, green, stinky, sticky, slippery, three, broken, hot, fast

pp. 74–75

The elephant sings.
The rocket launches.
The alien lands.
The monster hides.
The girl chases the monster.

pp. 76–77

What	When
Who	How
Where	Why

p. 78

wakes	runs
eats, cleans	laughs, hears
pets	feels

p. 79

stepped	stuffed
traveled	returned
looked	opened
grabbed	handed

p. 80

shoes	sweaters
mirrors	books
backpacks	computers

p. 81

St. Louis	United States
June	Lewis and Clark
the Gateway Arch	Cardinals

p. 82

Can I have a cookie?
Look out, Jack!
I left my hat in my room.
Hooray, it's snowing!
What's for dinner?
I have a dog named Pete.

p. 83

Circle the following:
We, Aunt, But, We, Tomorrow, I

p. 84

Sprinkles on run, look
Cherries on top of dog, book, ice
More frosting on pink, sweet, fast

READING

pp. 86–87

snake, scales, legs, hands, tongue

pp. 88–89

elephant, gray, huge ears, wrinkly skin, long trunk
wrinkly, pick up leaves, spray water

pp. 90–91

loves, smaller, four, six, thumb, Yes

pp. 92–93

Bronte, island, warm, cold, tall buildings. Answers vary for circle one and draw a picture.

pp. 94–95

excited, happy, surprised, frightened, proud, mad, guilty

pp. 96–97

candy shop, jelly beans, popcorn, a tower, no

pp. 98–99

Seven feet
He's afraid of it.

pp. 100–103
Mule, Pig, and Mole outside

p. 104
Answers will vary.

WRITING

pp. 106–107
explain, persuade, narrate, inform

pp. 108–109
Answers will vary.

pp. 110–111
Answers will vary.

pp. 112–113
Answers will vary.

p. 114
Mars, rocket, rocks, wheels, arm, water

p. 115
Answers will vary.

pp. 116–117
Answers will vary.

pp. 118–119
The plane flies in the sky.
The bus drives from stop to stop.
The boat sails on the ocean.
The bike rides down the street.
Answers will vary but sentences should reflect that Rafael walked or took a bike; Maja took a boat; Tía took a plane; and Adela took a bus.

pp. 120–121
Possible answers:
The bat hangs upside down.
The cheetah runs fast.
The monkey eats fruit.
The hyena laughs. What is so funny?
The crocodile swims in the river.

pp. 122–123
There goes a firetruck.
There goes a penguin.
There goes a train.
There goes a baby.
There goes a chicken.

p. 124
Answers will vary.

p. 125
Rolf is a furry wolf.
Don't scream! He doesn't want to be scary.
He has sharp teeth.
He uses his teeth to eat juicy apples.
Sometimes he feels quiet and shy around new people.
Being a friend makes Rolf a happy wolf.

pp. 126–127
Drawings and stories will vary.

p. 128
Circle the following:
Dr, edith, thank yuo, fluffy feles, better, you, grate

ADDITION AND SUBTRACTION

p. 130
7; 4 = 5; 3 = 8; 8 = 10

p. 131
1, 4, 5
3, 1, 4
5, 2, 7

p. 132
4, 5, 9
3, 2, 5
1, 5, 6

p. 133
5
9
7

p. 134
4, 3, 7
7, 4, 11

p. 135
7, 3, 10
4, 8, 12
cookbooks!

p. 136
Second row line to 7
Third row line to 9
Fourth row line to 10

p. 137
5
5
8

p. 138
6
6

p. 139
3
4
5
2
6

pp. 140–141
Answers will vary.

p. 142
6
8
10
12
14
16
18
20

p. 143
Quarter line drawn to 25 cents
Three pennies line drawn to 3 cents
Two nickels drawn to 10 cents
Dime, nickel line drawn to 15 cents
Two dimes drawn to 20 cents

p. 144
8 + 5 = 13
10 + 4 = 14
8 + 9 = 17

p. 145
10 + 6 = 16
12 + 5 = 17
11 + 7 = 18

p. 146
Column 1: 9, 15, 14, 10
Column 2: 13, 14, 12

p. 147

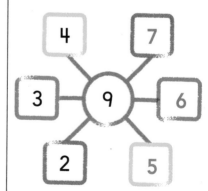

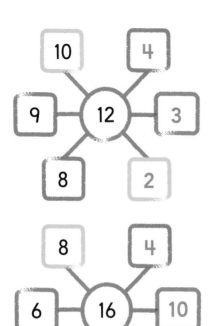

pp. 148–149

First page of spread: 10, 17, 5, 20, 15, 8, 12, 9

Second page of spread: 11, 13, 11, 16, 14, 10, 7, 10

p. 150
7
4 = 4
3 = 3

p. 151
4, 2, 2
6, 3, 3
5, 4, 1

p. 152
6, 1, 5
4, 3, 1
8, 4, 4

p. 153
8, 5, 3
10, 5, 5

p. 154
10, 4, 6
10, 0, 10
10, 6, 4
10, 5, 5

p. 155
3; 6 - 3 = 3
5; 7 - 2 = 5
5; 9 - 4 = 5

pp. 156–157
6, 3, 3
7, 5, 2

pp. 158–159
First page: 5, 0, 4, 1, 10, 3, 7, 1
Second page: 6, 1, 2, 6, 3, 3, 4, 2

p. 160
2; 8 - 6 = 2
1; 5 - 4 = 1
3; 8 - 5 = 3

MATH FACTS

p. 162
Guitars: 3, 3, 1, 2
Drums: 5, 5, 3, 2
Maracas: 2/4, 2/4, 4/2, 2/2

p. 163
Hamsters:
12 - 5 = 7 *or* 12 - 7 = 5
5 + 7 = 12
Guinea pigs:
5 + 6 = 11 *or* 6 + 5 = 11
11 - 5 = 6

p. 164
1. 3, 3
2. 6, 6; line drawn to 6
3. 4, 4; line drawn to 4
4. 5, 5; line drawn to 5

p. 165
-, +, +, -

pp.166–167

pp. 168–169
11, 4, 12, 6, 2, 8
Answers will vary. Possible answers include:
12 - 7 = 5 / 5 + 7 = 12

16 - 9 = 7 / 9 + 7 = 16
11 - 6 = 5 / 6 + 5 = 11

p. 170
21 - 3 = 18
15 + 6 = 21
18 - 9 = 9
100 + 20 = 120

NUMBERS AND OPERATIONS

pp. 172–173
Draw lines to:
1 jersey ⟶ 1 ball
2 jersey ⟶ 2 balls
3 jersey ⟶ 3 balls
4 jersey ⟶ 4 balls
5 jersey ⟶ 5 balls
6 jersey ⟶ 6 balls
7 jersey ⟶ 7 balls
8 jersey ⟶ 8 balls
9 jersey ⟶ 9 balls
10 jersey ⟶ 10 balls

p. 174
2, 4, 6, 8, 10

p. 175
10, 12, 14
16, 18, 20

p. 176
3, 4, 7, 9, 13, 14, 15, 18, 19, 22, 23, 24, 26, 28, 29, 33, 36, 39, 40, 41, 43, 44, 48, 49, 53, 54, 55, 58, 60, 62, 64, 67, 69, 71, 72, 75, 77, 78, 87, 88, 89, 90, 92, 95, 96, 99;
14

p. 177
5, 10, 15, 20, 25, 30, 35, 40, 45, 50, 55, 60, 65, 70, 75, 80, 85, 90, 95, 100

p. 178
Draw lines to:
3 nickels ⟶ 15 cents
5 nickels ⟶ 25 cents
2 nickels ⟶ 10 cents
6 nickels ⟶ 30 cents
4 nickels ⟶ 20 cents
1 nickels ⟶ 5 cents

p. 179
10, 20, 30, 40, 50, 60, 70, 80, 90, 100, 110, 120

pp. 180–181
10, 10, 10, 10, 10, 10, 10, 10, 10, 10
20, 40, 50, 70, 80, 90

pp. 182–183

Down 5 Less column:
5, 20, 35, 0, 75
Down middle column:
80, 60
Down 5 More column
15, 30, 45, 10, 65
Down 10 Less column
7, 23, 22, 39
Down middle column
70, 28, 32, 49
Down 10 More column
27, 43, 80, 38

p. 184

Clock 1: 1, 3, 5, 7, 9, 11
Clock 2: 12, 2, 4, 6, 8, 10

p. 185

5 odd
1 odd
3 odd
6 even
4 even
2 even

pp. 186–187

2, 8, 6, 1, 4, 10
1, 3, 13
3, 8, 38
2, 5, 25

p. 188

2, 7
6, 3
1, 8
5, 1
3, 9

p. 189

Draw lines to:
3 dimes ⟶ 30 cents
5 dimes ⟶ 50 cents
2 dimes ⟶ 20 cents
4 dimes ⟶ 40 cents
1 dimes ⟶ 10 cents

pp. 190–191

1, 6, 16
3, 2, 32
4, 9, 49
5, 4, 54
6, 1, 61

p. 192

less than, less than, more than

p. 193

>, >, <

pp. 194–195

> > >
> > < >

pp. 196–197

4 ones + 4 ones ⟶ 8 ones ⟶ 68
3 ones + 2 ones ⟶ 5 ones ⟶ 85
5 ones + 1 one ⟶ 6 ones ⟶ 76
3 tens + 5 tens ⟶ 8 tens ⟶ 85
2 tens + 5 tens ⟶ 7 tens ⟶ 76

pp. 198–199

53, 90, 53, 65, 65, 0, 81, 98

p. 200

Answers will vary. 8, 10, 15, 7

MEASUREMENT AND DATA

p. 202

3, 5, 7

p. 203

Answers will vary.

p. 204

1 tally sheep dog
7 tallies sheep
5 tallies pigs

p. 205

5, 3, 9

pp. 206–207

3, 4, Red Racer
Green Gust, Red Racer, Blue Bullet

pp. 208–209

10, 11
10, 11
13, 11
9, 7
11, 12
11
0
Answers will vary.

p. 210

Answers will vary.

p. 211

Draw lines to:
Hour hand ⟶ 10
Hour hand ⟶ 2
Hour hand ⟶ 8
Hour hand ⟶ 11

pp. 212–213

Draw lines to:
11 o'clock ⟶ 12 o'clock
1:30 ⟶ 2:30
2:30 ⟶ 3:30
4 o'clock ⟶ 4:30
6:30 ⟶ 7 o'clock
8:30 ⟶ 9 o'clock

p. 214

top clock, bottom clock, bottom clock

GEOMETRY

pp. 216–217

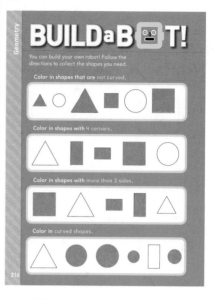

pp. 218–219

beans ⟶ circle
block ⟶ square
tissues ⟶ horizontal rectangle
cereal ⟶ vertical rectangle
square, circle, triangle or rectangle

pp. 220–221

12
down middle of square ⟶ make two rectangles
a cross in the middle of square ⟶ make four squares
a line down middle of diamond ⟶ make two triangles
a cross in middle of diamond ⟶ make four triangles

p. 222

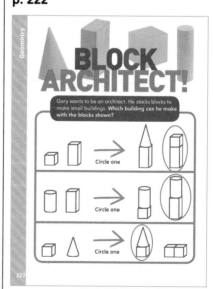

p. 223

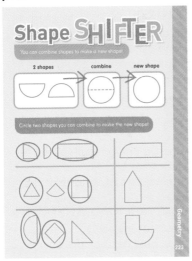

p. 224
left shape
right shape
left shape
left shape

p. 225
rectangle, circle, square, square

p. 226
apple, pink wafer, pie
Draw a horizontal line.

p. 227
Circle:
1st row: right
2nd row: left
3rd row: left
4th row: right

pp. 228–229
Answers will vary.

p. 230

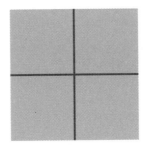

NATURE OF SCIENCE

p. 232
smell, hearing, touch, taste, sight

p. 233
Answers will vary.

p. 234
guinea pigs ⟶ balance
goldfish ⟶ thermometer
critter ⟶ magnifying glass
pizza ⟶ ruler

p. 235
~~scissors~~
~~rolling pin~~
~~binoculars~~
~~hammer~~
~~beaters~~
~~wooden spoon~~
~~shovel~~
~~screwdriver~~

p. 236
Answers will vary.

LIFE SCIENCE

p. 238
fish
bird
mammal
insect
reptile
amphibian

p. 239

	Walk	Swim	Fly
duck	x	x	x
butterfly	x		x
mouse	x	x	
fish		x	
bat	x		x
penguin	x	x	
parrot	x		x
alligator	x	x	
cow	x	x	

Ducks can move in all three ways. Another way animals can move is to climb.

p. 240
skunk
prairie dog
beaver
tarantula
clownfish

p. 241
Tree sapling, baby birds, flowers, and bunny should be circled.
Rock and fire should have x's on them.
Drawings will vary.

p. 242
X It moves less.
X It eats less.
X It drinks more.

p. 243
Circle the following:
feathers, beak, wings

p. 244
Drawings will vary.

p. 245
Answers will vary.

p. 246
1. grass
2. cricket
3. toad

p. 247
The following words or pictures should be circled:
water
sunlight
soil
watering can
sun

pp. 248–249
The following pictures should be circled:
cotton swab, wool socks, clay pot, wooden toy, book, ruler
plastic milk jug; plastic bag

p. 250
Designs will vary.

EARTH SCIENCE

pp. 252–253

Dear Elda,

I am writing to you from Earth! There are many different places to live!

I visited a rain forest. It is a wet environment. Birds and monkeys live in the (tall trees.) I saw a monkey eat a (bug!)

I also visited a desert! It is a dry environment. I saw a Gila monster! It lives (below the rocky ground.) It ate a (small bird!)

xo, Stella

Postcards will vary.

p. 254

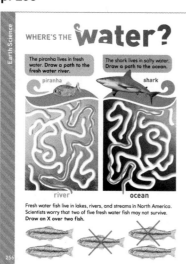

p. 255

We use air to breathe.
We use plants for food.
We use water to drink.
We use soil to grow food.
We use animals to produce food.
We use rocks to build things.
This book is made from paper, which is made from trees.

p. 256

WHERE'S THE **water?**

The piranha lives in fresh water. Draw a path to the fresh water river.

piranha

The shark lives in salty water. Draw a path to the ocean.

shark

river

ocean

Fresh water fish live in lakes, rivers, and streams in North America. Scientists worry that two of five fresh water fish may not survive. Draw an X over two fish.

p. 257

Big salmon should be circled.

p. 258

Answers will vary.

p. 259

Answers will vary.
Draw lifejackets on the people in the boat

p. 260

air
land (and sometimes water)
water

p. 261

Rex reduces.
Rory reuses.
Rayna recycles.
Answers will vary.

p. 262

In year 7 a farmer should plant cotton.

p. 263

bikes / air
trash / water
cans / land

p. 265

clockwise: spring, summer, fall, winter

p. 267

Answers will vary.

PHYSICAL SCIENCE

p. 268

star, moon, sun

p. 269

flip flop, solid
glass of juice, liquid
inside of balloon, gas
inside of bubbles, gas
bike, solid
contents of bathtub, liquid

p. 270

push
push
pull
push

p. 271

The ambulance siren, smoke alarm, and lifeguard whistle should be circled.

p. 272

mixture
dissolve
mixture

COMMUNITY

pp. 274–275

States and maps will vary.
The land pictured is mountains of Virginia.
Answers will vary.

pp. 276–277

Are you hungry? Go west of the couch.
Beware! Do not go south of the couch.
What time is it? Look north of the couch.
It's time to watch *Downton Mice*. The TV is east of the couch.
Water should be near the clock.
Pillow should be drawn between the mouse and the television set.

pp. 278–279

The park is on Strawberry Street.
The library is on Apple Avenue.
Circle two houses to right of school.
Drawings will vary.

p. 282

Symbols of the United States are:
American flag
Bald Eagle
Liberty Bell
Statue of Libery

p. 283

The oldest flag has 13 stars.

p. 284

Happy Martin Luther King Jr. Day!
Happy President's Day!

p. 287

The calendar shows May.
Thursday
Tomorrow is May 7.
Yesterday was May 19.

p. 288

Our flag has stars and stripes. It reminds us of the freedom we have in our country. Sometimes we fly the flag when we want to honor a hero for doing something brave and important. Some heroes are honored with landmarks that we can visit. This landmark honors President Lincoln.

p. 289

A hero stands up for equal rights.
A hero protects people, animals, and Earth.
A hero invents things to make life safer or easier.

p. 290

Circle leash.

p. 291

Answers will vary.

p. 292

A coach tells the team how to play.
A lifeguard tells swimmers how to be safe.
A mayor is in charge of a city.
A teacher tells students what to do.
Answers will vary.

p. 293

The ranger keeps plants and animals safe.
The police officer makes sure people follow laws.
The firefighter stops fires.
The teacher helps students learn.
The president is the country's leader.

p. 294

X Do homework
X Recycle

p. 295

I hope the pig won!

p. 300

Teri's timeline shows five days.
Teri did not go to school on Monday. It was President's Day.
She played soccer on Tuesday.
Teri brought cake to school on Wednesday.

On Thursday, she went to the dentist.
The last thing on the timeline happens on Friday.

p. 301

Places, schools, and transportation change over time. In the past, kids dipped pens into ink to write. In the present, we use pens. Technology helps people travel faster and more safely. It also changes how we communicate, or the way we share ideas and feelings.

p. 302

Lay out two pieces of bread.
Spread peanut butter on one side piece of bread.
Spread jelly on the other.
Put together for a delicious sandwich!

MARKETPLACE

p. 304

Draw line:
I can fix your car / mechanic
I can clean your teeth / dentist
I can drive you to school / bus driver
I can take your dog for a walk / dog walker
I can cut your hair / barber

p. 305

There are 13 goods.

p. 306

[ ] Take dog to vet
[X] Get dog food
[X] Get dog toy
[X] Get new collar
[ ] Take dog to groomer
Answers will vary.

p. 307

Dale sold more blueberry muffins than any other flavor.
Dale sold three baskets of oat bran muffins.
Banana is the least popular flavor.
Altogether, Dale sold eleven baskets.
Dale sold 110 muffins altogether.

p. 308

Answers will vary.

p. 309

Amy sells lemonade.
Amy buys a plant from Albert.
Albert pays Tina to fix his car.
Tina buys lemonade from Amy.

p. 310

Answers will vary.

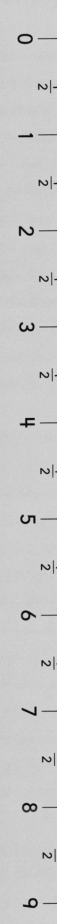

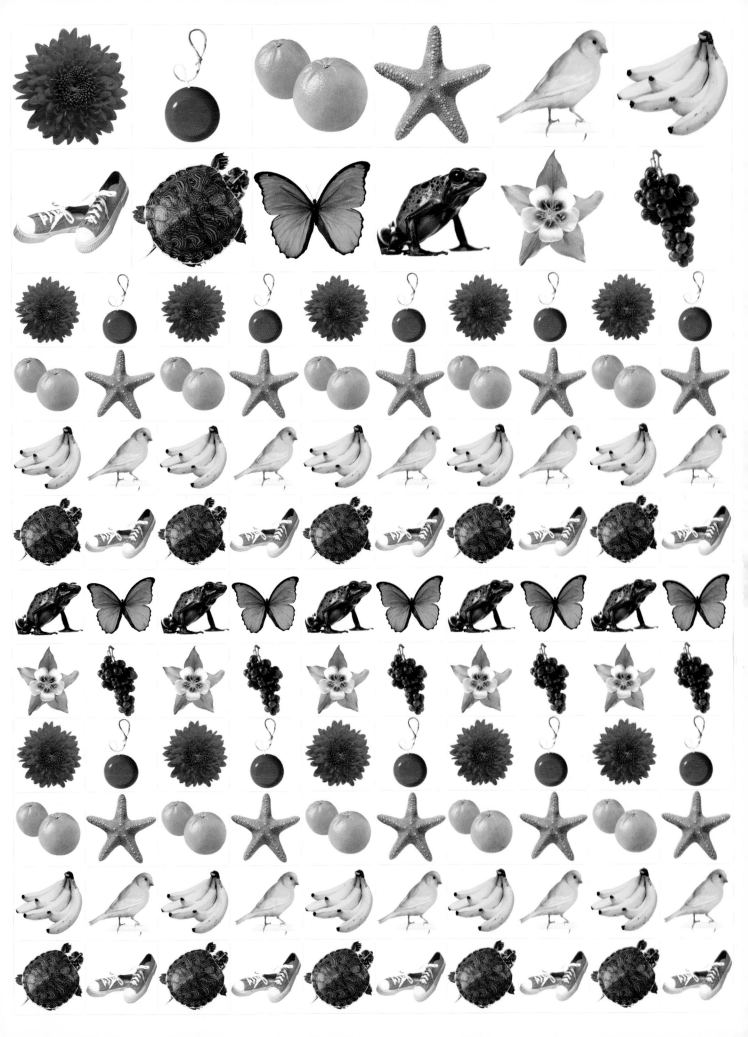